First Edition

Smart English:
Kick-Ass Lesson Plans

TEFL Discussion Questions & Activities

– China

Part 1 *Intermediate*

Andy Smart

Kick-Ass Lesson Plans - TEFL Discussion Questions and Activities China – Part 1
Copyright©2012 Andy Smart. All rights reserved.
Cover Images© 2014 Andy Smart
Illustrations © 2013 Andy Smart
Logo Design © 2014 Andy Smart
Lesson Plans © 2013 Andy Smart
Devil's Advocate as a spoken/oral English activity in EFL/ESL lessons © 2013 Andy Smart.
Power Activities in spoken/oral EFL/ESL lessons © 2013 Andy Smart.

ISBN 978-0-9926912-5-7

Permission is granted to copy or print anything in the 'Printables' section in each lesson plan. These are also available for printing from the supplementary book 'Smart English TEFL Discussion Questions & Activities – China. Complete Book of PDF Printables'.

No other part of this book shall be reproduced or transmitted in any form or by any means, electronic or mechanical, including photocopying, recording, or by any information retrieval system without written permission of the publisher.

First Edition published by Andy Smart 2014

About the Author

England
Born in the UK, Andy Smart has been a qualified teacher since obtaining his PGCE at the University of Brighton in 1990 and has been involved in education ever since. In England he taught at secondary school level for many years and was also strongly connected to work with SEN students including those with severe learning difficulties. This focused on integrating them into mainstream classroom activities in order to achieve their GCSE's and 'A' levels. Later, this commitment led to the establishment of a new day centre and an accompanying curriculum for people with autism. Moving to management in further education, his primary role was in finding placements to meet SEN students' individual requirements aswell as setting up and running various outreach projects.

From there Andy's involvement shifted to supporting EBD students who had been excluded from school. His work aimed at guiding young people back onto a pathway, safe from the negative influences of modern society. During this period, his team successfully created a specialised centre for their students' education, fostering the skills needed to survive in the outside world.

Asia
In 2005 Andy relocated to China where he began teaching English to adults in the city of Guilin, Guanxi Autonomous Region. From there he moved to South Korea working in Seoul, teaching young people at academies and also giving private tuition to teenagers in their homes. Returning to China in 2007 he started work in Beijing creating a strong network throughout the city. Since then he has been primarily involved in teaching his spoken English lessons, delivering lectures and training.

In many ways this book is a culmination of years of practice in the classroom. Drawing from a diverse background in education and extensive practice during his time in Asia, Andy has been able to develop a successful learning package aimed at people who want to improve their oral English skills. This is a strong and effective system that promotes fluency, confidence and accuracy, building a platform where the learner comes away with a high level of self achievement. Students therefore start to perceive English in a different manner, instead regarding it as a natural part of their daily life rather than a separate entity that is an ongoing struggle

Contents

Preface: Five Types of Teacher

Introduction: Teaching Great Spoken English Lessons

1. **Office Management**

2. **Your Students**

3. **The Teacher**

4. **Classroom Management**

5. **About the Lesson Plans**

6. **During Class**

7. The Lesson Plans

Part 1: People

1. Age
2. Personality
3. Feelings and Emotions
4. Personal Appearance
5. Parts of the Body

Part 2: Relationships

6. Family
7. Friends
8. Romance and Dating
9. Marriage and Divorce
10. Parties

Part 3: House and Home

11. Houses and Apartments
12. Describing Objects

Part 4: Daily Life

13. Shopping
14. Clothes and Fashion
15. Banks and Money

16. Giving Directions

17. Numbers and Quantities

Part 5: Food

18. Food

19. Cooking

20. Eating out

Appendixes

Appendix A. Grammar at a Glance

Appendix B. Using Phonetics

Appendix C. Common Student Errors

Appendix D. Quick Fire Activities

Complete Book of PDF Printables

Preface

Five Types of Teacher

It's always fantastic when you get positive feedback, so when one of my students came up to me and said

"Andy, why do we love your classes so much?"

I immediately felt like a million dollars. You can't beat praise to bring you up at any time of the day and it's one of the things that you never get tired of hearing. It's not a brag; we all have things we are good at. I've been teaching for years and it's my specialism; that's all there is to it. A hands-on role in the classroom is one of the things that I've always done best and love doing.

To me the formula for a teacher's work satisfaction is a simple one:
- Seeing your students improve and the accompanying look of achievement on their faces
- When they are successful in reaching their targets
- Developing an excellent rapport with them
- Planning your own ideas then seeing them come into fruition in class

Prep-work has always been my strong arm. Thinking well ahead doesn't only lead to great lessons; it normally adds an extra dimension that raises standards even higher. Indeed good prep work has so many positive knock on effects that a committed teacher will spend their career developing their own extensive library that they can refer to at any given notice.

Though I've been developing these lesson plans since moving overseas, the essence of how I teach hasn't changed from when starting out way back in 1990. To me the key to success has always been through confidence with which we can create our greatest achievements. This is the most fundamental law that applies to education. We can have the greatest latent ability, but without confidence we will never be able to realise our full potential.

I won't go too overboard, but really, if you are interested in your students coming back for more on a regular basis than have a bash at these lesson plans. There are no guarantees; the single most important and deciding factor to any great class is entirely dependent on the mood, character and willingness of the teacher. However, if you go in to it with a smile and your energy levels high you should have no problem.

Five Types of Teacher
There are five types of teacher that could use these lesson plans:

- Already established teachers who may be looking to freshen up or add to their existing material. If your career is in education then keeping your lessons from becoming stale is an essential day to day element. You have to stay ahead of the game and be continually searching for new ideas and approaches, especially if you are attached to the same students for any length of time. The activities here are guaranteed to jump start anyone's spoken English lessons back to life with an accompanying bonus of feeling energized once again.
- New teachers coming to China. This includes people who have no teaching experience and just want to leave their old life behind. Often you will be thrown in at the deep end and find yourself suddenly teaching with little or no form of induction. Luckily once you have taught your first class you will realise what an incredibly nice job you have just started and how brilliant your students are. Use these plans to help you settle in and bring you confidence to your new start.
- IELTS and TOEFL teachers who also have to deliver a spoken English package. Many find themselves scratching their heads as to what they should be doing instead of their normal highly structured approach. Most are trained to deliver classes which are 90% teacher talk time with students taking notes.
- People who are backpacking and may be invited to do some teaching while they are on the road. If you are touring China then teaching is an ideal way to get closer to this unique culture. Not only will you find out more about the education system, you may well be invited out to dinner, evenings out or even activities to areas of interest that most tourists won't see. Having been pencilled in to teach, it may be difficult planning from a hotel room or dormitory so in this respect these plans are ideal.
- Foreign students who are studying in China. Many English speaking students also want to work part time to supplement their allowance. Most don't have time to prepare properly for class while they are immersed in writing a dissertation, so in this respect these plans are important time savers.

Introduction

Teaching Great Spoken English Classes

Teaching English has been big business in China for sometime. If you are looking to teach English in the PRC then the most common areas fall into these categories:
- Kindergarten
- Middle and high school
- Business English
- Teaching spoken English to students who want to study abroad.

For me, by far the most rewarding form of teaching is the last one on the list. I admit that teaching kids at any level is a wonderful job having taught in many secondary schools in the UK. If this line of teaching interests you then fire away by all means. There are endless positions available in China, especially in Kindergarten. You just have to be driven, patient, extremely energetic and absolutely love kids to do this line of work.

If you can attach yourself to a good company as a regular then business English is also a nice job, though is certainly a hit and miss affair until you find a stable platform to work from. You can spend endless hours travelling to each company; time that you don't get paid for. When you arrive, your class will consist of professional people who are more focused on dealing with the mountain of paperwork on their desk than being in class. They are often there because their boss told them, not because they really want to be. If you have to deliver a package of lessons to professionals it had better be damned good.

Spoken English at English Language Training Centres
On the whole, if you are wondering which is the easiest and most comfortable line of teaching to get into in China, it surely has to be teaching adults who want to study overseas. This is the focus this book and from now on all references are made accordingly.

There has never been a better time to cross the water and set up shop in China as a teacher. In recent years, the market has expanded to new levels and business is clearly booming. 'English language training centres' (ELTCs) have sprung up across the country as millions of students seek to further their education abroad. Some companies are now so big that they are more like teaching supermarkets packed to capacity, buzzing with hundreds of students and staff. ELTCs offer a lucrative package with an astronomical price tag that is seen as an investment by the parents. You name it they will sort it for you; most importantly your visa application and also finding suitable colleges by their ranking. Of course the higher the ranking the better chances of landing a decent job when you come back.

The root of this lies with the fierce competition in the Chinese job market, where taking a master's degree on home soil won't count for much if you are looking for a reasonable position. There are so many people job hunting that the only way to make it is by using everything you have in your arsenal and then some, so going abroad for further education is the most desirable thing to have on your CV. Often there will be six times as many people attending job fairs than there are jobs, especially with the waves of college graduates that are available each year.

The Ethos of Spoken English Classes

Colleges in Western countries give conditional acceptances to non native speakers. A student must get the required scores in either IELTS which stands for the International English Language Testing System or in TOEFL, the Test of English as a Foreign Language. Both are split into reading, writing, listening and spoken parts each contributing towards an overall total. The age old problem that Chinese students have, lies in early education where speaking is largely ignored. Through continual repetition, dictation and testing children learn a huge vocabulary yet don't get the chance to practice using it. They can pass the written and reading part of their exams no problem, but when it comes to being able to string a sentence together their ability is often surprisingly limited. In this respect, the role of the English teacher is not necessarily as a 'teacher' in the literal sense, rather than someone who is able to unlock their students' passive ability.

These lesson plans are specifically designed for students to realise their potential and is done through fostering the fact that they have already done the hard work at school. At the end of the day, the key to the whole thing lies in growth through confidence and less about learning new things. Watching the transition from having a quiet individual who is unable to say anything to someone who becomes the centre of attention in class is most satisfying. I often wish that my Chinese speaking levels could improve so quickly but then of course I've only just started from scratch, whereas my students have been quietly learning English for years.

Kick-Ass Lesson Plans: Interior

This book is a complete package for spoken English that you can take with you into the classroom, delivering great lessons that your students will love. You can simply march into class and use the lesson plans directly, with the only prep work needed being to look at the plans for half an hour the night before. You have the option to print off information if you don't want to spend too much time on the white board and also there are couple of topics where a projector would be desirable but these are not essential. Accompanying the plans is a step by step guide plus valuable tips on teaching outstanding lessons leading to a strong professional approach if you are new at the game.

Students will soon appreciate that when coming to your class, they will be receiving a strong package aimed at improving their spoken English. Not only that but they will also have a thoroughly enjoyable experience at the same time. Good humour, crazy power activities and arguing aside though, from the teacher's point of view you will be in total command of the lesson, observing and managing your two hours with confidence and satisfaction. From the moment your students walk through the door to when you clean the white board before going home, you will have set up an effective learning platform from which they can all advance.

This book contains:
- Twenty 2 hour lesson plans for conversational English, covering most topics used in IELTS, TOEFL and daily life.
- A simple 'how to' guide and breakdown of the lesson structure.
- Back up information to support you which comes with each topic in the teacher's notes. This may be general knowledge about the topic, or something specific, for example, T17: Numbers & Quantities has conversions between measurements. This may also be in the form of tips on how your perception of the topic as a foreigner may differ from that of your students.
- Additional questions and activities in case you have to teach the class again within a short time frame. These are especially useful if you are a full time teacher with a regular schedule.
- Worksheets and printable information. This is meant to save you time and energy from writing questions and activities on the white board. There are also flashcards, though you will be required to cut them out with scissors or guillotine.
- For the newcomer to TEFL there is advice on how to teach professionally with a high degree of excellence.
- How to manage your classroom efficiently, maximizing the degree of learning by your students.
- A list of common mistakes that Chinese students make with their spoken English.
- For those who aren't quite clued up on grammar, there is a grammar survival guide that has all the basics in black and white at the end of the book. It is easy to follow and can be used at the drop of a hat to answer any grammar questions that may come your way. Just hit 'search' to find what you want.
- A phonetic table and chart; a really useful thing to have at hand when teaching spoken English. The study of pronunciation and its transcription into phonetics is practiced and understood by most Chinese students.
- Advice on office Chinese office management and how things are done differently than in other countries.

When you can use the lesson plans

Scenario 1
English language training centres will usually provide a text book for you to use. This is the most likely situation that a teacher will be faced with. Sometimes it may be the company's own model written by someone within the organisation or its own data base of lesson plans which you should print off beforehand. More than often though, they may use a well known book that is readily available on the shelves of most bookstores or purchased online.
However, classes in China can last up to two hours so the reality is therefore, how on earth can you make their material last for this amount of time? If you have to use a text book, after half an hour your students will already become bleary-eyed, looking at their watches or most likely drawn to their mobile phones with a painful sigh. If you are using material provided, you may well find that it is woefully inadequate to cover the distance, with its content equally as lacking. If you persist in using these resources for the whole two hours there is a big chance you will get negative feedback from management as the student said you class was boring.

Use these lesson plans to tack on to this type of class. The topics in this book cover just about everything that you will find in any text book or material you will be given. Use the company's material for half an hour and then switch to these lesson plans. You can say you have fulfilled your requirements and the students will walk out having had a thoroughly entertaining and useful time feeling very positive.

After a few lessons there is a chance that your students will not even want to open the required text book and you can use these plans from the very beginning. One huge drawback of nearly all text books is that they have a very limited number of chapters. If you have the same students for two weeks or more you will find that your text book will quickly run out and you will be wondering where you should go next. One time, much to the anger of my students, I was even told to start the text book from the beginning all over again as a review. Remember, your students have paid for their lessons and expect a professional job every time.

Another great draw back of text books is their attention to detailed grammar. Remember your students have spent years studying grammar at school. Even if they have problems with their grammar, most will want to steer clear of it and pay attention to reaching fluency with what they already have. It's far more effective to focus on your students individual problems rather than spend half an hour on something that many will already be familiar with.

Scenario 2
VIP classes: This means you will be teaching 1:1 in a small space, sometimes a cubicle with a small table, two chairs and a small whiteboard if you are lucky. The student will have paid a huge amount of money for their two hours, which for you could feel like an eternity. You will of course be provided material, though it may not have been written by a teacher. Use their material until you feel the need to switch to these lesson plans. No

doubt there will be something here that will fit back to back neatly with the topic that you have been given. Use the discussions and activities that best suit the situation including the additional material.

Scenario 3
Another very common way of teaching is called 'The English Corner'. This is more like a drop-in where students will come in and out informally and just have conversations to practice their English. This may be down a coffee shop, down the bar or just back in the classroom with an open door to anyone to mosey on by. If you are doing this, chalk up one of the topics a week in advance and have the plans in your hands or up on your laptop ready to go.

Scenario 4
Ideally, you will be given a free hand in what you can do in class. In this case you will easily be able to set yourself up and establish yourself as a great teacher within the company using these lesson plans almost instantly.

You can also propose to your management that you want to develop your own spoken English lessons, showing them these plans and how it could be a new initiative within the company that no one else is doing. Having been in and out of various offices in China for years, I know that this would definitely raise a few eyebrows. Talk about promoting the classes with leaflets and posters. Remember that English language training centres are primarily about business. If there is the possibility of making money then your management will take it on board.

1 Office Management
in English Language Training Centres

If you are an established teacher who already lives in the PRC then by all means skip the next few chapters and head straight for Chapter 5 'About the Lesson Plans'. If you do decide to have a nose through though, no doubt at some point you will be biting your lip as you empathise with some of the less desirable scenarios which are described.

For anyone who is on their way across the water to start afresh then these next few pages should be extremely helpful in terms of settling in then establishing some kind of rhythm and balance to your working life.

I remember one time when a nearby company asked me to deliver a one month business English package to professionals for them. They gave me the relevant text books and I planned accordingly. Upon arrival on the first day, I slowly made my way through a horde of around thirty parents and their excited children on the way to the classroom. When I got there, there was no one around who looked like they were there for the class so I went back out into the din to ask what was happening. The woman at reception knew nothing about the business English class. Looking fairly surprised she was immediately on the phone calling her superiors who came to the office in an instant.

They had cancelled the business classes and booked a month's worth of elementary level classes for young learners without telling me. With absolutely zero plans and an accompanying heart attack, I made up the class as I went along while parents and staff all watched intently. Many of the kids were so shy they wouldn't talk and some couldn't speak any English at all. Luckily I always keep a world map and one of the UK in my bag along with paper and pens, so at least I had some way to create a working atmosphere. After two extremely long tiring hours I was more than happy to hand my text books back and say goodbye to yet another company who were unable to communicate.

I do find myself continually scratching my head as to why this is the case; it's not rocket science after all. It's hard to put your finger on how and why things are done so differently in a Chinese office. There are some fundamental management skills that should be in place no matter where you are in the world yet if you are working for an English language training centre in the PRC you will quickly find that this is not the case. Normally the larger companies will run a fairly tight ship but the moment you start moving down the ladder, practices which one wouldn't expect to find on home soil appear with regularity. There are a number of contributing factors to why things can go pear shaped. Maybe it's a case of too many managers or perhaps a case of a culture that's trying to expand too quickly while cutting corners.

Either way, prepare to be mega flexible when starting out. After a while you become accustomed to the once a week helping of mismanagement that will be awaiting you when you walk through reception. The best way to go into it is by explaining via examples so here is a brief rundown on what to expect.

Unannounced Classroom Changes
I am a continual advocate of altering your schedule so you arrive at your classroom half an hour early. There are many reasons for doing this for all teachers any time any place, but it really applies in China. Often you will find that your classroom has been changed and no one has told you about it. This doesn't necessarily mean you can just move into the new one with no hitches. A new classroom means you may have to rearrange the tables, that there are not enough chairs, there may be rubbish lying around with faulty or no equipment. You may find that the classroom is the bottom of the barrel and really unsuitable. It may be the smallest one with a tiny white board and your students all squashed in like sardines. In this case, having gone in early you will have given yourself enough time to sort out the problem.

Last Minute Changes
One common occurrence is for someone to be calling you asking you to do something at the last possible second. Things can also be cancelled in this manner, even while you are on the way to your venue. Cancellations and changes can often be done via text message instead of a call.

Broken Equipment
Once again, another reason for getting in early is to check that everything you need for your class is there and it works. It's for this reason these plans do not rely on Power Point and only two topics in the series need a projector; Art and Festivals, though even for the latter a projector is not essential. Computers that have been used for years by countless others should never be relied on and must be checked well in advance. If you are early and your computer isn't behaving then you can move to a classroom with one that works. If you need a CD player, then check the office has one and it is up to standard. If your whiteboard is broken or too small then take one from an empty classroom that is not in use. No doubt your students will all want to help you move it.

These lesson plans give you the option of using material that can be printed out and photocopied. Most copy machines have the knack of breaking down just when you need them in any country, so I personally never ever rely on office equipment. You can use nothing other that the white board for all these plans. Printables are included here purely for your preference.

Thrown in at the Deep End
As a newcomer, you would expect to go through some induction period to become familiarised with your new environment. In China, this is often just the opposite. You may find yourself suddenly teaching classes without really knowing what you are doing. You may also be asked to do other activities which can be quite overwhelming if you are also just coming out of a hefty dose of culture shock. As someone whose feet have only just touched the ground, insist you stick to a single set of lesson plans and that you get a few days induction. This could come in the form of classroom observation where you can sit in on someone else's lessons and get an idea of how it's done.

Text Books and Other Material
You may well be given a text book to work from. A company must be seen to be putting some form of material on the desk in front of the students; it is a business after all. Normally they will choose from a standard set of well known books which most companies use. Each chapter or topic will be no more than a few pages of speaking, listening via CD, reading, some multiple choice questions and basic grammar focus, (the CELTA course, or Certificate in English Language Training for Adults, is a great way in learning how to maximize what you can do with these text books). If you have to use the text book for two hours then you have your work cut out as you need to keep your students enthusiastic and interested at all times. Your company may provide you with material from their own database though you may well find this to be also limiting.

Noise Levels: There is always some form of building going on wherever you are in China. If you are teaching you may find workmen banging away next door or the floor above. It may actually be your own company that is responsible for the noise, where once again no one has told you about it. In this case simply go outside and tell someone to wait until you have finished teaching and they will stop the noise no problem. If it is an outside source then this is another great reason to get to class early so that you can move to a quieter location.

Other Activities
A newbie will often be asked by other departments to do all sorts of one off things. You may well get asked to do them at the very last minute so if you are new to the game then learn to say 'no' quickly (see below). They may be unorganised and eat up half of your day. Combining them with your already existing schedule can be a headache which will leave your batteries dry. You may also be doing business with another department, in which case you will be then getting paid two separate wages. These other activities may come in the form of:
- Demos: A free class that will promote the company. Some of these are advertised and you will find your picture up on posters and fliers all over the place. Some are

'walk-ins' where during a large event, prospective students can come and sit in to have a listen. In any event, make sure that you get advanced warning of demos and plenty of guidance as to what you should be doing.

- Lectures: Similar to demos except there will be a larger turnout. You never know what to expect so once again, get there well in advance. I've been to lectures where they give you a massive introduction and when you walk on they play music. Many teachers dislike doing big demos and lectures. The more people there are the less you will get anyone to interact. Instead you get a sea of blank faces who don't understand your Western jokes.
- Parties: Christmas, Thanksgiving and Halloween are all times when your company will be on the hunt for people to run various parties for the students. Even if you love running this kind of event, after a while they can become tiresome, especially as they require so much effort. New people are always the first to be asked as they haven't developed the knack of saying 'no' (see below). In extreme forms, you may have to get up on stage in front of a crowd and become the entertainer. Just remember that these are merely promotions for the company. You are being paid by the hour and its work.
- Business English: If your company covers a broad spectrum of education there will be a department which deals with corporate training. These people are continually on the hunt for foreign teachers to do some work for them and are adept at selling themselves. There are some golden tactics that are employed in these circumstances. The most common one is to change the goalposts once you have agreed to do something. This may be by saying they made a mistake and the hours suddenly double. You may arrive to find that you aren't really teaching in the office. Instead someone is waiting to take you to a corporate building across town and they are late or can't find it. This sort of thing can destroy your day while only being paid for a few hours for the effort.
- Tests: You may be asked to sit and listen to students for half an hour to assess their ability leading up to their IELTS or TOEFL exams. This is ok if they are included in your schedule back to back with one of your classes so you can make the hours up. If it's a one off, ask yourself if you really need to be doing it?
- Teaching kids and college students at school or on campus. Many ELTCs accept work from external sources so you may get asked to do some work offsite.
- Teaching IELTS classes. You will normally be asked if you have a high academic background. IELTS classes are 90% teacher talk time, where students listen and take notes. Lessons can be two hours long and the teacher has to be very well prepared with Power Point and have a strong lesson structure. These lessons focus on methods of raising your score when taking the IELTS test.

Positives: Start as you mean to continue

It's easy to get past the mismanagement; after a while you just get used to it. If things don't go to plan, then normally it's only the foreign teacher that's having a heart attack trying to sort it out. Actually your students will just happily sit there without complaint until class gets going and may struggle to understand why you are getting worked up. Office staff will treat whatever issue that arises casually with no raised voices or gaskets being blown. In these situations it's pointless getting stressed out about anything as no one else does and you will certainly get absolutely no negative feedback from your superiors.

There are also some huge advantages which swing everything back into balance. Remember there are thousands of established teachers who enjoy a comfortable, relaxed and really interesting lifestyle for the following key reasons:

- There is no stress. This relates to workload but also your financial outgoings.
- Full time is considered to be 80 hours a month. That's four hours a day for five days a week!
- You can often choose your own hours, when you can and can't work including mornings, afternoon and evenings. The larger companies have set hours, but generally with other English language training centres you can give them your own requirements.
- Choose the location if there is more than one office.
- Choose what you want to teach.
- Your students will be really great with no behavioural problems.

Manage your Schedule

If you're new to China then from the outset keep your schedule simple. Ask for regular hours with no running around between venues. Tell management that if possible you would like to do at least four hours a day in the same office. Ultimately it's up to you to manage what you do. If you aren't happy about doing something, then don't do it. As a newcomer you will asked by many people to do different activities in different places. My advice is to make sure that what you are doing is as straightforward as possible with your time placed in manageable chunks. You can then start to enjoy your free time, exploring your new surroundings. You're in China after all and it's not all about work!

Make sure that you tell your management what you want to teach and what you don't want from the beginning. Check your contract before you sign it. If it includes other activities that you really don't want to do then say before you sign on the dotted line. They may not be able to change the contract if it is a standard template. Normally though, management will give you their word that you will only teach what you have verbally agreed on. You can always refer to this when the schedule is being done or if someone asks you to do something you aren't interested in. There is a general process of acceptance that applies to us all. This only takes place if you don't put your foot down and determine what you want to do. If you allow the process of acceptance to run its course then you will end up doing things you really dislike doing. Be strong!

Notice that the teachers that have been around for a few years aren't the ones running around between offices doing bits and bobs. They have regular hours, a familiar schedule and routine.

Saying No

One thing that has taken me years to get used to is saying 'no' to doing extra work that's not on the schedule. I'm sure it's an inbuilt Western mechanism. From past experience, back on home soil it's difficult to say no when the manager asks you to do something on top of your normal hours. If you can to talk your way out of that one, then the next time you are asked you really feel an obligation to do it. The boss may well develop negative feelings towards you if you don't work the extra on a regular basis.

In China, if someone asks you to do something that isn't covered by your schedule, it is seen purely as an opportunity for both parties to earn extra money. If you say you don't want to do something then that is as far as it goes; they put down the phone and just ask someone else; its business plain and simple. There are no bad feelings or repercussions so try and cut out that annoying ingrained feeling of obligation.

2 Students

As a teacher your primary goal is to do your absolute very best for your students with the main aim being their improvement in whatever field you are working; in this case it is in spoken English. If they have a test of some sort, then your target is also in ensuring that they attain the correct score so they can go abroad. If it is for a professional who needs to speak English at work, it is making sure they leave armed with whatever they need to communicate with Western colleagues and clients effectively.

I was speaking to one of our longest serving IELTS teachers the other day. As per usual we ended up comparing the different styles of lesson and how they related to student ability. Whereas my classes focus on the students talking, the IELTS classes are nearly all centered on the teacher doing the work. Indeed the students just listen, watch Power Point and take notes for two hours on exam preparation. IELTS grades range from the Band 1 classed as a 'non user' to Band 9 who is an 'expert user'. Most students fall somewhere between the 5.5 and 6.5 bracket. TOEFL is scored on a scale of 0-120 points, though the speaking test is computer based.

I asked him if his hands were tied when it came to the class interacting and practicing speaking. "Actually, for the Band 6 and 6.5 classes, if I ask my students to speak in English most will be unable to talk for longer than a minute. After that they will go quiet just sitting there doing nothing. If we try any form of speaking practice, I have to quickly move on and get back to myself doing the talking. The simple problem lies in that they don't learn how to speak English at school. It's not that they don't practice the basics. They drill lexis over and over and learn grammar in the same way. The trouble is that's as far as it goes. They never learn how to develop an argument or conversation in any shape or form".

It always strikes me as odd when a student's note making ability which may be impeccable, in no way matches their ability to verbalise what they have just written. The education system in the PRC instead focuses on reading and writing facilitated by tests and more tests. A student may have a good command of grammar and an extensive vocabulary especially if they are doing IELTS or TOEFL which demand that what you learn is often well outside of what a native speaker uses in daily life. Your students may have already done extensive ground work before they walk through your door. When I did my CELTA language certificate, my teacher advised all of us

"Never try and teach your students grammar. If you do, you'll find out that they will probably know more than you and you can make yourself look really stupid. If you need to explain something, put it up on the white board and let them do the explaining for you."

The Keys to Successful Spoken English

With all the ground work already done for you, your role is therefore slightly different from the normal perception of what a teacher should do. Your job is merely to create a pathway to encourage putting what they already know into practice. You are there to assist your students unlock their passive ability that's been growing since they started school.

After a lifetime of acquiring so much unused knowledge, I can only imagine its like learning to drive for years and years but never buying a car. To most, the key to speaking is a secret that is tantalisingly just out of reach.

80% Student Talk Time

Firstly, get them speaking as much as possible. Really you should be aiming at 80% of the two hours dedicated to your class speaking, not the teacher. Remember, that for most of your students this will be the very first time that they will have had the opportunity to start speaking in English, let alone interacting with others. Roll your sleeves up each lesson and get on with it while remembering not to do too much of the talking yourself. They are paying to learn to speak after all. The bottom line is, if you get them speaking they will inevitably make some degree of progress.

Discussion

Also remember that you are not delivering grammar exercises from a book. They've seen it, done it and need to see another text book with the words 'grammar focus' like a hole in the head. Make all your activities geared towards one single aim and that is interacting. Most of the work in these lesson plans is done in pairs. Unless stated otherwise, assume that your students will be interacting using spoken English with their classmate. Again, this will be a new thing for them, something that is clearly visible if they are first timers to your class.

Some students may be able to articulate spoken English to a fairly high level. This is fair enough, but you may discover that they have been learning text virtually word for word in order to pass their IELTS tests. There are countless books which offer an 'ideal' model answers which should be used to attain a good score. Unfortunately, one of the first things any examiner will be listening for is someone who has rehearsed their dialogue. If this is the case, IELTS examiners may ask a more difficult follow up question to see if this is the case. Follow up questions are also included with these lesson plans to familiarise your class with this.

The material included here, allows the students to step away from a model and start expressing themselves in their own way. In terms of spoken English it encourages movement away from standard text book English. In the real world we use English which is far simpler than in any test. To instill the self-belief in someone that what they already know is enough to attain fluency is like handing them a golden ticket in confidence.

Chinglish and Bad Speaking Habits
The term 'Chinglish' refers to the direct translation from Chinese into English. It's hard to get away from doing this; it's an easy mistake to make when learning any language and often it can set someone back a long way if these bad habits are particularly ingrained. The route of the problem, once again can often be traced right back to the very beginning. Young learners are taught from Chinese English teachers who it seems have little grasp of practical usage. One of the most common errors you will hear from every single one of your students will be "How to say?" instead of "How do you say (something)?" or "How can you say (something)?" In this sense, the job of the spoken English teacher seems easy; it's just a matter of ironing out all the creases and getting your class to understand the error of their ways. The real obstacle though, is getting past something so habitual that having identified a problem, the individual will immediately forget everything you have just said in the blink of en eye. Consequently you will find that your mature students who are in full time employment may be the hardest cases to work with. On the other end of the scale, as more and more parents are investing time and energy in their child's education, a student who is still at high school will often be already speaking pretty good English.

A page of common student problems is provided in Appendix C.

Confidence
It can't be restated enough that confidence is the single most important that you should be nurturing with each one of our students. It is the one guiding factor and pillar throughout these lesson plans and should be at the back of the teacher's mind at all times when communicating to their class members.

Confidence confidence confidence is what it's what it's all about! From confidence comes fluency and from fluency we become even more confident. It's a wonderful cycle of growth ending in success. There are many ways in which you can focus specifically on confidence building. Here is a checklist of what you could be doing. Most of these will be reiterated somewhere later in the book.
   • Firstly you need to create an environment that will facilitate the confidence building process so your students can break out of their shell. To do this you need to create a friendly and relaxed atmosphere. As a teacher, always be positive in class from

the moment you walk through the door. Smile and keep your energy up. Your mood and approach will be picked up by everyone else.

- Arrange your space so that the tables aren't regimented like a normal classroom.
- Write your students' names on the top of the white board before you start your class in order to match up with where they are sitting. There are a number of reasons for doing this. In this case it is so you can aim questions at specific people. If you ask a question to the class as a whole, you may either get zero response or the most outgoing student answering all the time. It is natural for most to sit back and say nothing.

You can therefore aim particular questions to students who you know may be able to answer. You can ask simple questions to quiet or lower ability students and more complex questions to the more able. For anyone, to be able to answer a question correctly in front of the rest of the class is a massive confidence builder. The opposite is the worst most counter productive thing you could do, so ask your questions mindfully. If someone answers correctly give them a 'well done' and a thumbs up, especially to new and quiet students.

- Say hello to all new students at the beginning of class. This has been included at the beginning of every lesson plan. Others will wait for five minutes while you do it no problem. Ask them what their hometown is, if they are a student or have a job? If they are a student, what are they studying? If they are working then what's their job? Why are they studying English? If they are going abroad, which country are they going to? When you are doing this, you are also secretly giving a brief assessment of their ability. From this, you can immediately start asking questions accordingly using their names which you have just written at the top of the white board.
- Positive visualisation: When you ask a student why they have joined the class they may reply "Because my English is very poor." In this case make sure you explain the benefits of thinking more optimistically instead of creating a self fulfilling prophecy. Give them a realistic alternative to say such as "My English is improving every day". Write it on the board and get them to copy it down.
- Remember your students' names. This sends out the signal that you care about them and therefore their progress. It demonstrates you are a professional committed teacher and your students will assume that in your hands their speaking ability will go forward. Keep a notebook in your bag so you can record the date of each lesson, the topic and names of who was there. Next class you can refer to this if you can't remember someone. There is nothing worse than asking someone their name again and again. If a student returns after a long spell away from the classroom you can refer to your book and miraculously remember who they are.
- Mixed abilities: This is always a contentious issue with teachers. Some schools make a conscious effort to stream their students but even so, at times you may find you will have a class ranging between the very able and the fairly limited. In this case try and organise where different students sit accordingly. A low ability student will immediately plummet in confidence if they are paired up with someone who can speak freely. More on this in 'Classroom Management'.
- Be mindful of how fast you speak. If it's too fast your class will collectively go through the following stages: confusion, shut down followed by inevitable boredom. If it's too slow, they will feel like they are in kindergarten again.

- Take your time explaining tasks and questions. If it means cutting out one of your discussion questions from the lesson plan then do it. Better that everyone shares clarity than confusion. Understanding and confidence go hand in hand.
- Sometimes, even after explaining a discussion question or activity as clearly as possible, someone may still not understand what they should do. Give the class time to warm up before they get going, it may even take a few minutes. Either way, slow down and bring your maximum patience to bear. Once they get it, it becomes another breakthrough in confidence.
- Allow your students to talk in Chinese with their classmates from time to time if they don't understand or can't remember something. This eases any pressure of having to know everything by heart.
- Move from table to table during discussions and listen in. You may choose to interact or even correct your students as they talk referred to as 'hot correction'. Be especially mindful when you are doing. Often you can inhibit someone who is making real progress with their fluency, potentially damaging their confidence. Instead you can also do a 'PACS' (Post Activity Correction Session) where you remember the problem and discuss it afterwards has finished using the white board to help.
- For new students let them settle in for half an hour before you approach their table. Remember that they may have never spoken to a foreigner before let alone actually be interacting in English.
- Lesson plans are structured gradually, starting with the easiest questions. This is so that your students will have gained in confidence, ready to attack the other activities and more complex questions after break.
- Many of the activities are based on argument and disagreement; I call them 'Power Activities'. We'll go into this later in 'About the Lesson Plans' but until then, lets just say that they are designed to keep students in quick spontaneous dialogue rather than thinking, translating and using their dictionaries. They are absolutely huge confidence boosters.
- Where a roleplay requires three or more people, one student may be required to take the lead. Make sure you don't throw a new student in at the deep end. Give them one or two classes before doing this.
- Point out one or two simple areas of improvement that they can focus on during the next week or so. With simple targets your students won't be overloaded, especially if they also have college or office work to think about. The difference between a 6 and a 6.5 in an IELTS test can be a matter of a few basic but regular mistakes.
- During the lesson, if one of your students has made noticeable progress over the course of their study with you then tell them before they leave to go home. Take notice of the ones who are starting to open up and become fluent. If a student has been visibly using your advice from previous classes to make improvement then also acknowledge it.

Keep in mind these points and try and instill as many as you can into the way you teach. If you really care about your students then these will quickly become second nature. Enjoy watching their progress.

3 The Teacher

Aside from your students making improvement ask yourself what do **you** want personally from your lessons and your life as a teacher?

The highest target you can aim for are the following:
- Knowing that your lessons are excellent.
- Great feedback from your students who say they love your classes and they can't wait until your next class, "See you tomorrow!"
- Great feedback from staff, especially management.
- E-mails from students thanking you and telling you how much they enjoyed your classes.
- A pay rise and permanent contract.
- More support from management when you want something done, either in the classroom or with legalities such as visas.
- Students will tell their friends about your class and what a great time they have been having; how they have improved easily and that they should also come to your class.
- Being part of a growing network of teachers and schools abroad.

In order fulfill these aims you need to be professional. This means:
- Being early.
- Being well dressed. In most cases for a guy, smart jeans and a shirt is ok.
- Smiling and giving off positive energy no matter what foul-ups were made by the staff five minutes earlier.
- Checking your schedule before you go out of the door. Go to the right venue and take the right lesson plans with you.
- Being well planned: You have these plans so that's the bulk of your work already taken care of. Make sure that people see you are well planned.

- Be focused on and committed to your students' progress.
- Be strict. I don't mean rule your class with an iron hand, just create an air that you are serious about seeing them progress.
- Monitor your energy levels. Teachers should pace themselves between holidays. If you put all you have into every class you will quickly run your batteries dry. It's also easy to get sick if you are a teacher as you are in contact with so many people all of the time. If you maintain your energy then you are much more likely to keep on top of things.

These may not seem like rocket science to many, but believe me, I've seen many teachers unplanned, untidy or come stumbling into class with minutes to spare or even late; something unacceptable in state run schools. Lateness is the one area of slackness that does not go unnoticed in any English language training centre though you will get a few chances to redeem yourself before you find you are no longer included in the schedule.

Just because things are relaxed with a more open atmosphere, there are still some invisible boundaries that shouldn't be crossed so you do need to be strict at times. Keep your students off their mobile phones and their attention towards the work at hand. The worst habit is when a student suddenly leaves class to answer their phone therefore abandoning their partner for five minutes while everyone else is talking. When they return, you may have started the next discussion and they missed the run in. You may have changed the pairings. If someone keeps coming and going it can be highly disruptive to the class. The worst is during a role play when they are taking the lead role. Try and fill in the gaps if you can. Be firm about this and the message will soon spread that it's not the done thing behind your doors. It also merely underlines your professionalism.

Being Early

Being early has many benefits if you are teaching in China. I always add half an hour to my schedule and make it the norm in my daily life. If you get into the mindset of going half an hour early then it immediately ceases to become a pain. It's far better to casually meander into work rather than rush there. It means that you can focus on extra things you could do to do to improve upon your lesson before you get there. Being early means:

- If someone has changed your classroom without telling you then it will give you plenty of time to find your new one and make an assessment of what needs to be done.
- You can rearrange the furniture so it suits your class.
- You can clean the white board.
- You can check your white board pens.
- You can check the computer and projector and get them working in advance. If they are broken you can move to a spare classroom.
- If need be, you can swap white boards and anything else from another empty classroom. Your students will no doubt be quick to help you with this.
- You get a chance to go over your plans one more time before class begins. This makes a huge difference, especially during the opening few minutes when you start teaching.

- Staff will see you are early and see this as a sign of professionalism. They will feedback this message to their colleagues.
- Students will see you are early and take this as a sign that you care.
- You will be able to sit students with matching ability together as they arrive. If they are already sat down before you get there, you therefore have the choice to leave them where they are or move them. You better have a good reason for moving them.

The Tone of Your Lessons

Chinese students have had a lifetime of the traditional classroom style of learning. Most find sitting in class an utterly tedious experience that they have no choice but to endure. The IELTS and TOEFL classes are certainly no exception to this so after listening to countless hours of the teacher talking it's the last thing they need when coming to your class.

Ask yourself which teachers do you remember most from when you were at school and why? Of course the ones that cared and brought life to your learning experience are the ones that stay with us forever. I remember staring out of the window during my most boring lessons. I even the recall view in detail but bear no memory of the teacher.

The first golden rule of any spoken English lesson is to give your students that 80% talk time (STT). It is therefore logical to expect that the teacher's amount of talk time is limited to 20% (TTT). With such an easy rule to follow it's surprising to hear of teachers talking far too much in class. What your students don't want is to listen to another teacher droning on and on. Some may even complain if you do it too often. It's also an easy mistake to make and from time to time, even after all these years I still find myself falling into the TTT trap. The sight of bleary red eyed students looking at their watches is a sure sign that you should drop everything immediately and get them talking as soon as possible.

Keep your lessons humorous and light hearted at all times. If something doesn't go to plan then brush it under the carpet; it doesn't matter. At times become the entertainer dropping in anecdotes for a few minutes before a discussion, especially things that have happened to you. Pick out discussions which allow you to do this.

Grab a catch phrase from somewhere you really enjoy saying. I remember one of my EBD colleagues back in the UK used to say "f<u>a</u>ntastic!" with a strong emphasis on the first 'a'. I love saying 'am<u>a</u>zing!' with emphasis on the second 'a'.

Most Chinese people live very conservative lives, even when they are at college. Some topics such as T10: Parties are an excellent vehicle to talk about how different our worlds are apart. Many will be going abroad soon and will be extremely curious of cultural differences, listening intently to anything you tell them about your life back home.

Many topics really require the teacher to have some background knowledge beforehand. This is included in an easy to read format in the teacher's notes. Refer to these notes and become a fountain of knowledge that will impress your class.

Your students have a great sense of humour. Remember that although they appear to be a fairly conservative bunch, they are still adults all the same. Don't be afraid to push the boat out a bit and have fun with them. Each lesson plan normally has some roleplay and the 'Devil's Advocate'. I call them my Power Activities as the level of fluency visibly picks up during these times. Both will be explained later in 'About the Lesson Plans'. Chinese students absolutely love argument and roleplay. They are generally very uninhibited during these sessions, taking great delight in playing out the various scenarios becoming far more outspoken. Often things may become fairly riotous. Other classes next door will wonder what's been happening. When the class has finished people will leave smiling and you will wonder where the two hours just went. Sit back and enjoy!

4 Classroom Management

There are many gains to be had from organising your classroom properly. It's not difficult; just arrive early and make an assessment of how you need to arrange your space and what you want to get out of it. Taking control of this important element of teaching shows people that you are in charge and you care about your lessons. Pride in your classroom reflects on your attitude towards your lessons and your students as a whole.

In English language training centres classrooms are usually practical affairs consisting of a white board, tables, chairs and hopefully a computer with projector and speakers. If the equipment doesn't work then you should have time to change it or move classroom. If the white board isn't up to par then grab another one from an empty classroom as they are very light.

Table Arrangements

A standard IELTS or TOEFL classroom will have regimented rectangular forward facing tables in lines (figure 1). If you get given a large capacity classroom with lots of desks then you have your work cut out. Best leave it be and not rock the boat with any office staff.

However, if your space is a manageable size with up to ten desks then get stuck in and arrange them to become more conducive to conversation rather than note making. Arranging the tables makes a massive difference to what you can do during class. Although the staff in reception may be scratching their heads as to what you are doing, remember that they are not teachers and have most likely never taught a single lesson in their lives. At the end of the day, you are responsible for your class. You are the one who will be standing in front of the students not them.

The best thing you can do with rectangular tables is rearrange them so that you form two rows so that your students are sitting side on to you. At least they can interact with their classmates sitting opposite aswell as next to them. You can also move freely around the classroom and visit your students personally. Another approach with square tables I've seen is to make a large C shape. This is ok, but it uses up a lot of space and the students are only able to converse with those either side of them. Also students have a tendency to sit in the corners where they are the furthest away from attention.

Sometimes there are no tables. Instead plastic chairs are used with small fold down writing boards. Though they are easy to move around, they are also very restrictive for the student to turn around and talk to others. They are also limiting when it comes to group activities. If you have a choice, don't use them in a spoken English class.

The best case scenario is to have round tables instead of the traditional rectangular ones as you can do so much more with them. You can fit three or four students around each one and they are still facing towards the teacher at all times. You can move around the classroom freely and visit students while they are talking. It's also easy to quickly change partnerships, forming group activities far more fluidly. Make sure students do not sit with their back to you.

Figure 1

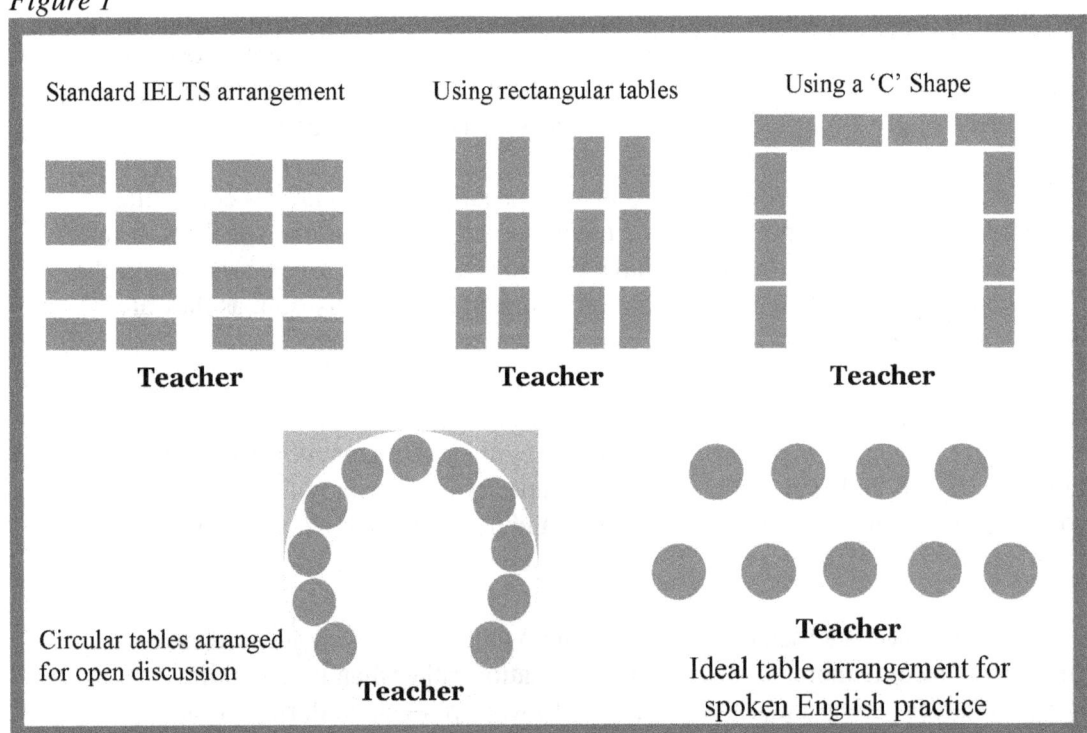

Beware of the temptation to form a circular shape for group discussion. I can understand the idea of having a debate but there are definite drawbacks to doing this. Unless the group is evenly matched you may well find that many will sit back and say nothing. While they are sitting there they will be feeling a mixture of negative feelings; pressure, nerves, resentment or blame towards the people who are doing all the speaking plus plain old boredom may swiftly creep in. Not only that, but no doubt someone's confidence just took a tumble if they didn't manage to contribute much. Normally one or two outspoken or higher ability students will dominate the proceedings. Remember, even if it was just one student who was sat there for half an hour saying nothing, then you have failed as a teacher. Your job is to be there for everyone not 95% of the class.

Mixed Abilities and Talking Partners

The age old grumble for many teachers is the pairing of students with different abilities and that there should be some form of streaming in place to avoid such inconsistency. Unfortunately, in the real world, even if your company has other classes which ensure people are placed more appropriately, you will inevitably still end up with two individuals sitting together who are at different levels. In this case it is the teacher's job to be mindful of the situation and do your best to manage it. Prioritise matching ability levels. There is nothing worse than two people who stop talking after one minute because they are not in sync'. Not only are they having a negative experience but their mood can easily bleed into the rest of the class.

Assuming you are familiar with your students, the key to it is being in class before anyone arrives and seating them accordingly as they come through the door. You can recommend that someone sits with a classmate who is more evenly matched in ability beforehand. If you need to make space, then ask people to move aside and add a chair for someone who would do much better in that seating position. "Can we just add a chair just here for Susan?" is an easy request to make that people will respond to no problem. On the whole, this is far better and easier than asking someone to move later. This can be really embarrassing and therefore confidence destroying.

Make sure people only sit at the back if there are no spaces left. Always encourage them to come up the front. You can hear what everyone is saying in the front row. You can therefore correct any outstanding errors they make and monitor discussions. People at the back have less concentration, speak more Chinese and also use their mobile phones.

If someone comes in late and they don't work well with their classmates, then bear in mind that at some point you will do some general changing of partnerships anyway. It's a great way of freshening things up since it completely changes the dynamics of the session. Be mindful of who you would like to change. Some people will need 'waking up' and swapping people is often just the jump start they need. It's a very straightforward thing to do. Simply pick two relevant people before the next discussion or activity. With your palms facing up, use your hands and outstretched arms to indicate who they are and what they should do, saying

"Could you two please stand up……..and now swap over please. Ok, and now sit down. Thank you very much". Job done!

Time Management and Lesson Structure

The key to a good lesson is your time management plus a good strong and simple structure that you can alter when the need arises. Luckily you have these here in your hands right now without doing any work. The table Figure 2 helps to demonstrate three common elements that run through every lesson plan and how they combine to focus on the learner. A detailed explanation of the different activities A-E is provided in 'About the Lesson Plans'

Figure 2

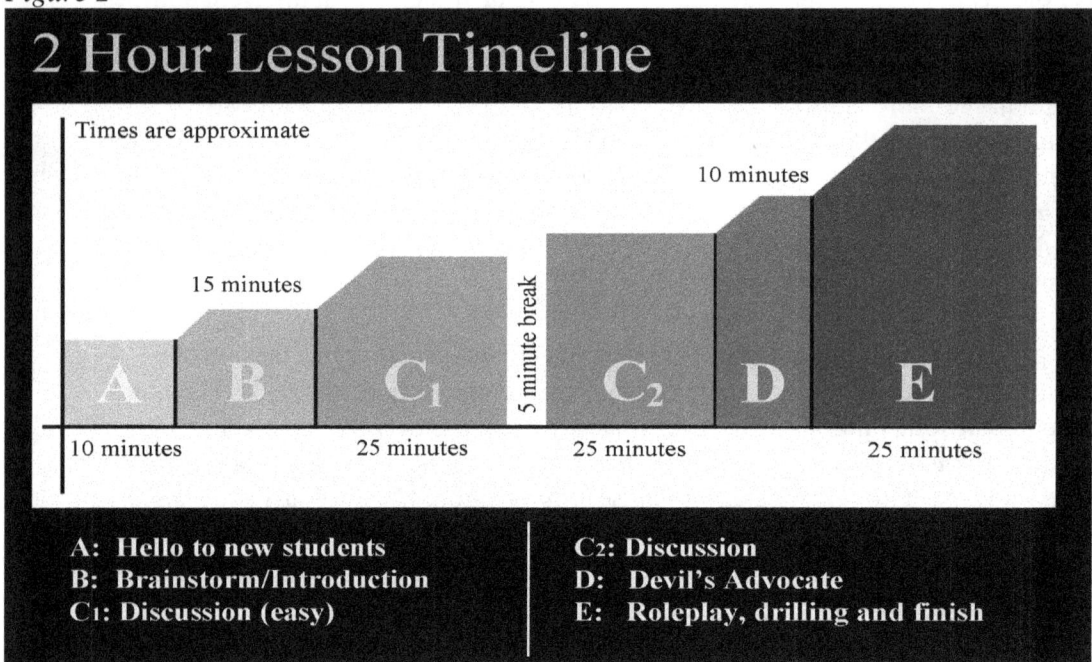

The three core elements are:
- **Timing of each activity**. Normally you will need five to ten minutes to say hello to new students and introduce yourself. Following this, around fifteen minutes to start the class proper. This is generally aimed at building interest in the topic. The main body of the lesson is based on discussion with a five minute break at the half way stage. In the latter part the Power Activities are introduced for at least half an hour.
- **Arrangement of activities**. Start with the essentials first. This should be a lead-in and then basic discussion practice. Often these are basic IELTS type questions giving students the chance to practice before a test. Sometimes they may come and show you something that they really need to do, in which case you can easily swap a ten minute slot for what they want. After break, discussions can become more complex, for example, T19: Cooking looks at whether or not you can cook? If not why not? If you can then what is your best dish? After break the focus turns to recipes and the cooking process. You can't hope for anyone to keep one hundred percent concentration for such a long period so the 'Devil's Advocate' is designed to snap students back into life with a ten minute bust of energy. This sets them up for the following roll play leading up to the end of class.
- **Noise levels**. In a spoken English class, you can easily tell how interested and absorbed your class is by the volume; a quiet class can indicate lack of interest or

understanding in your objectives; in my opinion, the noisier the better! If you have a good lesson, then even the lower ability students should be conversing by the latter part. The vertical scale in Figure 2 is measured via levels of interaction, attention, fluency and noise. Lessons start quietly with the introductions and the lead-in A and B. Be mindful of keeping your lead-in too long. Being intuitive between activities is a really useful tool an experienced teacher uses as second nature. As the class moves on, activities are designed to encourage heightened interest and participation, escalating to a point where your students will become very vocal towards the end. Aim your sights at your class really enjoying their English and having as much fun while speaking as much as possible.

Managing Your Whiteboard

Your white board is the most useful, reliable and important tool you have in the classroom. You may find that the electrical equipment may either have been borrowed without your knowledge or broken, completely shelving the bulk of what you planned to do. If you need to use the computer, over head projector, speakers or CD player make sure well in advance that everything will be in there and in working order before you get there.

These lesson plans take away this element of uncertainty, allowing you to focus one hundred percent on the content of what you will be teaching. I rarely use company computers as most of the time they don't work properly or it takes time to get everything working. If all else fails then you always have your trusty whiteboard to fall back on to.

Figure3

| bus, coach (mode of transport) | **Transport** | Jennifer, Jane, Tony, Xiao Wei, Joe, Hai Xia, Wendy, Helen, Rachel, Sara, Michael, the teacher's name |

bus, coach   (mode of transport)   **Transport**   Jennifer, Jane, Tony, Xiao Wei, Joe, Hai Xia,
the London Underground   Wendy, Helen, Rachel, Sara, Michael,
the Tube   the teacher's name
carriage   this
compartment   that
transfer   PAST TENSE   those

bunk bed
~~top bunk~~   Describe your longest journey   thought
~~middle~~   thankyou
~~bottom bunk~~   When did you go?   thanks
                                     Where (*did you go and from where*)?
sleeper train   Why?   commute
overnight   Who with?   commuter
                                    How long (*did it take*) ?   traffic jam
                                    Did you transfer? (*Which vehicles*)? grid lock
                                    What did you enjoy about it (*or not*)? road rage

                                                                                              aggression
                                                                                              aggressive
                                                                                              aggressiveness
                                                                                              aggressor

I know many teachers who don't use the whiteboard much but there are many advantages of becoming familiar with it. For a start if you write the discussion questions on the board, every student will be able to take their time understanding your aims clearly. If you just deliver aims verbally then many class members will understand only a percentage of what you have just said. You can underline key points or vocabulary and change the way you want to word the question or activity until it is as simple and effective as possible.

Figure 3 shows how you can maximise the effectiveness of your whiteboard. Start by writing the names of each student in order of where they are sitting up in the top right hand corner. In the centre write the topic. You can remove this later to gain some space on the top of the board.

Make a list of new vocabulary down one side of the board. Use the other side for pronunciation focus, word forms and other notes that can be referred to during discussion. Be sure to keep only useful information that the students can use throughout the lesson. Often this will be something that they don't need to write down, rather just use as a prompt during activities.

Keep the centre of the board open for writing discussions, questions and other activities at all times. At breaktime, take a couple of minutes to tidy it up, erasing things you no longer need, making things smaller, moving vocabulary, neatening things up and thus creating more space.

To help illustrate and elicit meanings don't be afraid to draw a few diagrams here and there. Even if you aren't great at drawing, it will be a light hearted addition to the tone of the class. My shark drawing is always terrible when I'm doing the topic on the sea and everyone laughs at it. Sometimes your white board can become somewhat of a masterpiece, for example, when I do 'Plants', people actually take photos of the board. (Both of these topics are found in Part 3 and the 'complete' version.)

Printables vs. the white board. Personally I would much rather use the white board to write up discussions and illustrate with diagrams. However, of course there will be many who won't want to go that far. For this sake, where discussions and roleplay require more than a minute's writing, a printable version is available to hand out to the students. This also applies to diagrams and illustrations.

5 About the Lesson Plans

Here is a complete breakdown of what you should expect to find in each lesson plan and how to use them. Though some differ from this standard template, overall you will still find roughly the same ingredients and formula in each one.

Vocabulary

A vocabulary list is at the top of every lesson plan.
Vocabulary can be single words or phrases. It may also be something we commonly use in daily life rather than something found in a dictionary.
The list consists of key vocabulary that may come up during the lesson.
Don't worry about trying to cover everything, especially when there is a long list. Just remember to work on the essentials. Try and bring some of these up during your introduction or brainstorming exercises.

Where there are alternatives, British English (UK) and American English (US) are included. Many students will pay attention to the differences, especially if they need to take a language test; IELTS is focused on British English while TOEFL is on American.

Write vocabulary up on one side of the whiteboard. Build lists during the course of the lesson that your students can refer to and analyse meaning, pronunciation and form where relevant. Make sure you drill key vocabulary at the very end to round off the lesson.

Timing

The plans are two hours long with a five minute break down the middle.
Each question or activity includes the time you should spend on it. Be mindful of overrunning and how that will affect those that are remaining.

Roleplays that are split into sections include the total time and the time that should be spent on each part in brackets.

The time allocated to each activity is based on the students' interest level and my personal experience teaching these topics. It's taken me years to get over my Western preconceptions of what should work and what won't work in class. You may think that a discussion on how unhealthy cigarettes are can be may last at least fifteen minutes but the reality is that some students may well go quiet after only five. Certain questions can hold attention span for longer than others. If a pair goes quiet they will sit there with a glazed look on their faces while everyone else continues. It may also create a domino effect where the class suddenly becomes muted.

Most questions are ten minutes long. This also applies to simple ones don't really develop into discussions. Time for introducing or explaining a question is taken into consideration.

Some questions are given more time to run a bit longer so not to fit too much in, giving the lesson some breathing space. If you end up with spare time then there is normally plenty to use in the additional questions if need be.

A: Hello to new students

Before class starts write the name of each student in order at the top of the white board. Make sure this is done in order according to their seating arrangements. This is especially useful in large classes. Underline the names of new students so you can refer to them quickly.

Saying hello is an essential start to any lesson. Welcome all your new students at the beginning of class. Others will wait for five minutes while you do it no problem. Ask them what their hometown is, if they are a student or have a job? If they are a student, what are they studying? If they are working then what's their job? Why are they studying English? If they are going abroad, which country are they from?

Talk clearly and carefully so new students can understand you, giving them time to answer. Remember that they will be nervous and very self conscious including professional people who have jobs. Often these will feel the most uncomfortable and awkward during this time. If they can answer you with no problems then this is a huge step in instilling an immediate sense of confidence. If they have problems understanding then encourage their classmates next to them to give a helping hand. At the very least you will have developed an instant team spirit.

When you are doing this, you are also secretly giving a brief assessment of their ability. From this, you can immediately start asking questions accordingly using their names written at the top of the white board. Remember, asking appropriate questions according to ability is an important confidence builder.

B: Brainstorm and Introduction

Here is where you introduce the topic. There are many ways in which you can do this. An easy run in to any class is to get your students to take turns brainstorming. Brainstorming means each person can say anything that springs to mind about the topic, be it one word or a phrase. Make sure everyone knows what it means before each class. For those who don't know, get one of the students who is familiar with the term to explain it to them.

The first few to do this will find it easy, but soon some may start finding it harder than they thought. It gets the obvious vocabulary out of the way and paves the way for more useful language that some may not be familiar with. Brainstorming does not rely on any visual material such as photos or Power Point to start things off. All you need is your white board. It is also guaranteed that each lesson starts off in a different way from the last time you taught the same topic. You may get things you never thought about before or those which are amusing, setting the lesson off with a good tone. One time we were doing the lesson on common health problems when someone thought of traditional Chinese remedies. I asked her to give me an example and she replied with "blood letting" leaving the class in stitches.

The key is to elicit as much as possible. Eliciting means the students give you information rather than you doing the work for them. There are some real positive gains to be made from eliciting:
- It is an excellent way for students to draw on the knowledge that they already have. If they do this is instills confidence.
- It generates an interest in the topic or discussion point.
- It focuses your class on a deeper level which they will take into the next task.

Get used to eliciting and make it second nature when you are explaining something, particularly during a lead in. Eliciting can be done in many ways for almost anything. You can do it visually with pictures, photos or a quick drawing on the whiteboard. You can use yourself and act something out. One of my colleagues could transfix the class with his eliciting skills. It's something that's really worth learning.

Hangman

On the CELTA, one of my tutors started his classes using a game of hangman and is another way to elicit your way into a topic. I've used this on many occasions since then as it always works really well. It also creates a relaxed atmosphere at start of lesson.

Apparently hangman is now considered politically incorrect. Don't worry about offending anyone with this game in China as it has no cultural significance. Students really focus on not being 'hanged' which has far more impact than any substitute. Don't worry about using the term 'hangman' either.

Make sure students put all their dictionaries on the table and keep their hands well away. If a student finds the word on their dictionary after you are half way through, it will destroy the activity.

C: Discussion

Unless stated otherwise assume all activities are in pairs.
If students are arranged in threes, larger groups or have to work individually it will be included in the lesson plan.

Write each discussion on the whiteboard so that the students can read it. Lower ability students will be able to take more time understanding all the aims. If you read a discussion point most won't be able to take it on board.

Selection of discussion questions are based on the following conditions:
- Usefulness for daily life, especially regarding Western culture.
- Usefulness for IELTS and TOEFL practice.
- Keeping a good balance for all students ability ranges within intermediate level.
- Maintaining a good level of interest.
- Keeping things fun and lighthearted.

There are also discussions which a native English speaker would find odd but work well with Chinese students, for example, 'What is the best age to get married?' Western people could probably find this question fairly pointless, with age not normally being a key concern. Chinese students however, will heartily jump into a discussion about this. The criteria for deciding a marriage partner is an engrained part of Chinese culture with age being near the top of the list. Because it is something so close to heart, your students will easily find it easy open up and express themselves. From this comes fluency followed by confidence.

Past and Future tenses
After all past and future tense questions there will be a reminder in brackets to underline its importance, for example

Describe your earliest childhood memory (past tense)

The most common mistake made by ninety nine percent of all your students will be with their tenses. Most continually speak in the present tense even if they are aware of the different verb forms. It's a habit that is easy to identify but difficult to erase. The only way to deal with it is to keep your ears pinned back and continually remind them. If a question demands talking in the past or future, call attention to this before they start talking, even using the quick fire activities in Appendix D to help focus on the work at hand.

Why or why not?
Many questions have 'why or why not?' written after them. This is a really important addition as it adds depth to what you are talking about. For example, if you ask the question 'Do you think it is better to be a vegetarian?' then half your class will finish the question without trying to develop it. You have to add 'why or why not?' after every question and stress that this is the key factor in creating discussion.

Topics in Brackets
After some questions or activities you may find other topics in brackets, for example

T1: Age. How many kids do you want? Boys or girls? (T6: Family)

This means that the question is repeated in T6. It is meant as a guide for teachers who are using the lesson plans regularly to supplement a curriculum and want to be mindful of doing the same question again, keeping an eye on the big picture. Some questions belong naturally in more than one topic so if you notice that you already did that discussion a week ago, then you can quickly jump to the alternative questions and activities and use something that fits in from there. There is nothing worse than a bored looking student saying they did that one the other day; it casts doubt on your professionalism and lowers the level of interest around the class.

Topics in brackets refer only to questions in the main lesson plan and not those found in additional questions and activities.

Please bear in mind that some discussions and activities may clash with those in Kick-Ass Lesson Plans - TEFL Discussion Questions and Activities China Parts 2 and 3. A thorough guide for crossovers runs through the length of the 'complete' version.

Underlined Vocabulary
Some things will be underlined, for example, 'Should a parent spoil their child? Why or why not?' In this case you should be asking them what 'spoil' means and its form.

Underlined words are a reminder that most likely you will need to take a minute or so to explain them. Make sure everyone in class understands your aims. Just ask one or two people by name what the underlined words mean before you start. If you just ask everyone as a whole they will all say yes and then immediately dive for their electronic dictionaries the moment you tell them to start.

Using Prompts
'Think of and describe three ways' or 'Think of and describe three types of'

Often you will come across a specific number attached to a question. If you just ask the question without a specific number, for example, 'Think of some two wheeled modes of transport' then most likely they will think of only one and finish talking after a minute or so. Adding a specific figure makes all the difference as does also asking the class to describe what they have just thought about. If they aren't absolutely clear that they should also make a description, then you will be given one word answers when you check later.

Breakthrough Questions (BTQs)
Sometimes it is ok to take prompting to a different level. Give yourself an extra minute when writing a question on the whiteboard with a list of reminders to help students

answer it in more detail. Give them some valuable starters that can make their conversations last a lot longer. Keep things simple and expand on them when you are explaining what to do.

I call these my 'breakthrough questions' as they generate so much confidence and self worth. They are marked on the most relevant questions accordingly. BTQs encourage extended student talk time, thus helping those with a lower ability to learn how to develop a topic. Instead of finishing speaking after the normal minute or so, they will suddenly realise that it is the teacher that's stopping them talking in order to move on to the next part of the class rather than them drying up. The gains from a well thought out BTQ are enormous. I try and add at least one in each lesson.

You would normally write a BTQ on the white board in this manner

'Describe one of your longest journeys.'
'Where, When, Why, Transfer, How long, Who with, Food, Sleep, Enjoy?'

While you are explaining it to the class, enlarge upon the above creating clear single sentence questions:

Where did you come from and go to? When was it? Why were you travelling?
Did you transfer and how many times? How long was the journey? Who did you travel with? What did you eat on the journey? Did you sleep while you were travelling? What did you sleep on? What did you eat? Did you enjoy it?

Some would argue that a teacher should instead be asking the students what these important points are rather then doing it for them. This has its merits, though at times you really need to generate a pace about your lesson. If the various prompts are already up there waiting for them, then they can just get on with it, after all what is there to be gained from wasting precious minutes asking them something they already know. In this case it is a form of over eliciting. Get momentum going in your lessons rather than creating unnecessary blank areas.

Follow up questions
These allow us to have a conversation in more depth and detail. If we don't use them, then things just become a series of questions that just skate on the surface of the topic. It also means that listening becomes equally as important as speaking, emphasising that a conversation is a two way interaction.

Certain topics encourage the use of follow up questions in order to develop an activity. The most direct way is to ask a question based on the last answer (**A<Q**).
Before starting, make sure your students know what they should be doing and lead in with an example. Ask one of them a simple question and then ask a follow up question immediately after. Get the rest of the class to think of possible questions with you, for example

Q: "How did you get here today?" A: "I walked." Q: "Why did you walk?"
A: "Because it doesn't take long to get here." Q: "How long?" A: "About 10 minutes."
Q: "How do you know it's only 10 minutes?" A: "Because I looked at my watch?"
Q: "What make is your watch?" A: "It's an Omega?" Q: "Why do you have such an expensive watch?" A: "I bought it in Switzerland."

Answer Checking

After a question or discussion you can ask one or more of the class to quickly go over again what their answer, ideas or opinions were. Even after a roleplay you can quickly debrief or simply ask what the outcome of their scenario was. Answer checking is essential element of any lesson in that it

- Reaffirms you care about what your students think.
- Underlines that your discussions are important.
- Reminds students that their teacher will be checking up on them and they need to have something worthwhile to say if they are asked.
- Sends out the message that you are a professional.
- Demonstrates that their lesson is structured and that they are getting good instruction.
- Trades effort with confidence if their answer gets a thumbs up from the teacher.

In theory you could answer check everything, but for the sake of time keeping and avoiding repetition, manage the number of checks that you do. Get that rhythm and energy going in class and make the clock move fast. Answer checks are added in the plans where considered the most useful.

Breaktime

Use this time to organise your whiteboard and create more space. Also think about how you will arrange people into groups for roleplay. You will also need to think about the Devil's Advocate which focuses on pair work. If you have an uneven number in class, think about how you can put two students together as a team versus a single student who is more outspoken and confident thus forming a group of three.

Use breaktime to focus yourself on raising the game to more energetic levels.
Have the next activity already written up before you restart the class.

D: Devil's Advocate (Power Activity)

This is a truly special exercise that will completely pick up the tempo and tone of the lesson and is an excellent warm up before the roleplay. I refer to it as a 'Power Activity' in that students become visibly stronger regarding their fluency and confidence within minutes of start-up. Power Activities are also a refreshing departure from regular classroom methods while still focusing on the spoken English and the relevant topic.

It's incredible what an argument does to unlock someone's speaking potential. The gains from your students engaging in argument are:

- Removal of the delay time in translation between Chinese and English. Interaction becomes spontaneous. Students focus on what they want to say rather than how to say it.
- Students don't use their dictionaries. This means that interaction becomes far more dynamic. Although dictionaries are very useful, they can also act as barriers to fluency. In this case, if the individual can't remember how to say something they will think of other ways to get around the problem via the use of already existing knowledge.
- Students have to use their listening skills in order to make a swift response.
- Students learn to break free from model text book English.
- A healthy atmosphere of interest, participation and enjoyment will spread throughout the class. The lesson will become noticeably louder.
- Nervous and self conscious students will break out of their shell, especially if they are seated with someone of a similar ability level.
- From fluency comes confidence and a strong feeling of self achievement. This will be visible when your students leave the classroom at the end of the lesson.

The one thing I've learnt over the years is how much my students love argument. Although argument for arguments sake may seem radical, trust that your class will take to the Devil's Advocate activity very well. Many will be controversial talking points, but don't worry about political correctness too much as they are always taken in good spirit. Some may be more appropriate in China, for example, 'Men should pay for everything on a date'. Most of your students would agree with this statement.

Take your time explaining this as it is doubtful anyone would have heard of this concept before. They wont be able to find it in their dictionaries either. Start by writing the title 'Devil's Advocate' on the white board. Next to it write 'I totally disagree with you' and then explain via example. Ask one of your students a simple question such as "Which country would you most like to visit?" Whatever they say, disagree with them and tell them the disadvantages of going there and suggest a different place to visit.

Further the demonstration by giving an example of something you would not normally disagree with. For example, if someone said they would like to visit the UK, I would be forced think of an argument against going there even though it's my home country. If someone said they loved football, I would have to take a side to the contrary even though it is my favourite sport. Once your students are familiar with this activity you will have no problem starting it off in following classes. If you have a new student, get someone else to explain it to them aside from yourself.

Playing the Devil's Advocate means that one student in each pair must construct an argument based what they know about something rather than their real opinion. Most will take the concept on board but there will inevitably be one student who will be unable to cope with it. In this case merely swap the roles within the partnership if it makes them more comfortable.

Example of the Devil's Advocate

T19: Cooking
Cooking is an essential skill that should be taught in middle school.   10 minutes

Put your students in pairs. After explaining the activity, delegate the argument to one person in every pair and that the other should disagree: "You think cooking is an essential skill. You disagree...You think cooking is an essential skill. You disagree...You think cooking is an essential skill. You disagree" and so on. Start things off with a loud and hearty "Go!"

Devil's Advocates are designed to be short five or ten minute exchanges. You will normally have to stop people talking in mid flow in order to make time for roleplay.

E: Roleplay

Chinese students love roleplay and are happy to take on board whatever part you give them to play in any scenario without inhibition. Most will become immersed in the task at hand so you can take a back seat and let them get on with it. Roleplay is an excellent vehicle for learning in that

- Skills that can be used in real life can be practiced and honed.
- Students can get valuable incite into Western culture.
- They further the practice of skills and knowledge learnt during class.
- They take away the pressure of set discussions, especially those aimed at IELTS and TOEFL.
- They encourage free speaking away from any set models found in text books.
- Students enjoy and have fun with speaking English.
- Great steps can be made regarding fluency and therefore confidence.

Sometimes you can keep people working in pairs but often you will need to take a hands on approach organising the class into groups. Always get the whole class to roleplay in small groups at the same time while they are seated.

Never get one group doing it while everyone else watches. If people are watching they are not talking and therefore not practicing their English skills. How long will they have to wait until it's their turn? Never get them to stand up and act anything out. This can be really embarrassing for the students concerned and fill the others with nerves wondering if they will have to stand up and do it aswell. Remember that the whole point is to instill confidence. There are three occasions in this series where someone must stand up in front of the class. These are:

T12: Describing Objects, where the class has to guess what the object is that the individual has taken from the bag. The student will have a large amount of vocabulary to help them on the white board and the teacher can support them if they are in difficulty. Sport: (found in Part 2 and the 'complete' version) where students must talk about their favourite sport for a timed two minutes. Though they don't have to stand up, they will still be the main focus of attention by the rest of the class.

Games and Gambling: (also found in Part 2 and the 'complete' version) where the class tries to guess the famous person. The individual only has to answer with 'yes' or 'no' questions.

Example of a Roleplay

T20: Eating Out
Person A: Waiter or waitress. Welcome your customers. Use Sir or Madame and be as polite as possible. Recommend the Chef's Special. Take their order.
Persons B & C: Customers. Order drinks and an entrée.

Roleplays are designed to be as clear and simple as possible. Roles are given as Person A, Person B, Person C and so on. Once you have put them into groups and explained the roleplay, go around the class delegating roles using your arms outstretched to signify who is doing what "You're A, you're B and you're C." This way everyone knows exactly what they are doing. Don't be afraid to do this in larger classes. Take your time organising it and when you are ready start things off with "Ready……..Ok GO!"

Some roleplays can be printed off so you can hand the different parts to each student, others should be written up on the whiteboard. At times you can use flash cards to help guide them through the activity.

If the activity requires someone to take a lead part then be mindful that the person you choose is up to the task. Definitely don't give the hot seat to a new student. Give them a few classes before giving them the task and allow them to become comfortable with their new classmates first. Remember to encourage the use of any notes and vocabulary on the white board that may be helpful during the session.
Some activities are based on practicing interviews either for work or on TV. These really promote the use of everything that was covered in class. For TV interviews the initials CCTV are used which stands for China Central Television.

Roleplay as a Power Activity
I don't often use games in my lessons, though you can find some in Games and Gambling (found in Part 2 and the 'complete' version). Games are great as long as they fit in with the context of the class. Roleplay as a Power Activity is designed to be as much fun as playing a game while sticking tightly to the topic and practicing spoken English.

I often create scenarios which depart from real life situations. These normally involve conflict or disagreement of some kind. Don't be afraid to have a go at these, even if they seem unorthodox. Once you see the effect that they have on your class you won't want to leave them out as they are so much fun. Once again, the transformation you will see from the quiet individual to an outspoken fluent speaker will be quite noticeable.

Many roleplays are set into two parts. The first is normally based on a normal every day activity such as buying or borrowing something. The second involves argument such as returning the bought item as it is faulty and asking for a refund. In this example the customers complain about the terrible food:

Part 1:
Person A: Waiter or waitress. Welcome your customers. Use Sir or Madame and be as polite as possible. Recommend the Chef's Special. Take their order.
Persons B & C: Customers. Order drinks and an entrée.

Part 2:
Persons B, & C: Customers. That food was terrible. Tell the waiter/waitress why. Refuse to pay the bill.
Person A: Waiter or waitress. It's not your fault. Make excuses for the terrible food. They must pay the bill.

F: Drilling and Finish

Debrief your class after the roleplay. There is no need to spend too long on this. Just make sure you highlight the strong players and those you thought made some kind of progress. If there were any errors you noted then do a post activity correction (PACS) on the whiteboard. You can also ask each group what the outcome of their roleplay was.

Finish off the class with drilling the most important and useful vocabulary on the board. Drilling basically means the class repeats the relevant target language after you do it. It is a nice combined effort where everyone is speaking at the same time harmoniously as one unit. It's a nice way to end.

Teacher's Notes

Where some advanced knowledge about a topic is beneficial for the teacher, a tab is available in brackets to take you to the teacher's notes, for example

Think of two wars (*teacher's notes*)
Which countries were involved? Why did they fight? What were the dates? Were there any winners?

Teacher's notes may range from general to specific information such as dates and measurements. Use these 'at a glance' facts and figures as reference and to become more knowledgeable on a subject, for example, which is the fastest man made vehicle? See T17: Numbers and Quantities (*teacher's notes*).

If you are interested in the topic then it will be one of the first things that rubs off on your students. This is particularly noticeable when delivering something like religion, plants or the environment. In some topics you will find a fairly large cache of information awaiting you. Be sure, that you won't be able to dump all this information on your students. Just try and remember one or two gems that can really add to the flavour of the lesson.
Often information is provided for the teacher's enjoyment as much as the students.

Printables

I have been using the white board during the whole twenty plus years I've been teaching so quickly writing up a question of any length for me is no problem. I even carry spare whiteboard pens in my bag. However, I fully understand that many teachers, especially regarding the roleplay, will look at them and think "no way am I going to write that lot out on the whiteboard". For this sake, if some things do require half a marker's worth of ink, then there will be a notification of a printable version in brackets, for example

E: Role Play: Advertise a product (*printables*)

There are also handouts and worksheets available which range from vocab' pages where you have to label diagrams, to flashcards, prompt sheets, questionnaires and some pages to handout before the end of lesson for your students to take home.

Look after your flashcards after you have prepared them. You will thank yourself next class you need them again. I keep mine paper clipped together and in sealable plastic bags in a box at home. This is especially useful if you are in the south of China which has a strong humidity and all paper gets wet. Remind the class to look after the flash cards, not to write on them and return them in good condition when the activity is over.

For the free ' Book of PDF Printables' copy and paste the code below and e-mail to smartenglish@hotmail.co.uk. This book is designed to be a helpful time saver for printing off the various worksheets, roleplays, handouts and flashcards. All the topics are bookmarked on the left of the screen so they can be accessed quickly.

SMARTENGLISH: A01 – SJY2568

Printers and projectors aside, the bottom line is that all you really need is the paperback, your laptop with an e-reader, a Kindle or tablet plus a white board to be able to use these lesson plans and still do a great class.

Additional Questions and Activities

If you have to teach the same topic again within the same month to the same class then additional material has been included. Also some questions naturally belong in more than one topic, so if you don't want to cover already trodden material then simply dive in to the additional material and choose something else. They are also there to use if you finish your class early. If so then you can always quickly grab something from this section. If you have a 1:1 class and you are unable to do the roleplay or Devil's Advocate then use this extra material instead. These are still all tried and tested material that just couldn't fit into the main lesson plans so they work just as well.

Student Book

I haven't used a student book in years. Really, there is everything in the teacher's copy to deliver sixty-six two hour classes with nothing other than a whiteboard at your disposal. In the case of maximising student talk time and participation in class, it is much more advantageous for eyes to be looking forward rather than to have heads down.

However, companies do like to provide material to give to their students. It is an unspoken rule that goes with any curriculum, increasing the sellability of any learning package on offer. We are given text books to look at when we start school and is an ingrained part of learning that goes unquestioned.

The student version is a lightweight version of the teacher's book with the bare bones of each topic. On many occasions in my early days of TEFL, I was given a student copy of whenever package I was supposed to be teaching with no sign of the teacher's book anywhere. In this case though, you will not be able to teach effectively using the student book alone.

If you are using the student copy alongside the teacher's book definitely have a look and see what is included and what you need to do before class.

Included in the student book you will find:
- All discussion questions and activities.
- All additional questions and activities.
- Vocabulary lists translated into Chinese which can be found at the back of each topic. This is to encourage students to remember and strengthen what they already know. They are meant only as a reference at the end of each class.
- A space to write down new vocabulary and expressions at the top of each lesson plan. This is to affirm new information, noted it down in the student's own personal way; far better than merely reading it.
- Some visual material. Check on what is included in the student book before you plan.
- A student guide on how to use the lesson plans including BTQ's, follow-up questions, Devil's Advocate and Roleplay.
- Common Student Errors as a separate chapter at the beginning of the book.
- The grammar and phonetic guide as appendices.

Not included in the student book:
- Timing of each activity.
- The second part of any power activity roleplay that is split into parts.
- Flashcards. Some things still need to be printed or written on the white board.
- Anything found in the teacher's notes.

General knowledge is there for the teacher to add flavour to the class, give spontaneously and use when and where they want. It's not meant as a heads down reading exercise which would break up the lesson.

6 During Class

Recently one of my students was just putting on his coat as he prepared to go home, when he turned to me and said

"You know considering these classes are two hours long, the time seems to just fly by in your lessons"

This was from one of my mature students who owned his own business, practicing English because it was his favourite pastime. Of course with the basic elements of the lesson structure in place you have already paved the way for a good lesson. However, there are many other things that you can be doing once the lesson has got underway in order to maintain a high level of interest and keep the momentum going. Once you have got accustomed to things, start to keep an open eye for opportunities to add some detail to the proceedings. Here are a few extra things you can inject into your class.

Visit Your Students

While they are involved in discussion, visit one of the groups and sit with them at their table. Join in the conversation though remember not to do too much of the talking. Students love getting a personal visit from their teacher. Many really want someone to listen closely to what they are saying and identify some of their problems. Some just really enjoy getting the chance to sit and chat with someone from another country. Make a mental note of any outstanding problems someone has with their English. If possible quickly write it down after you have left the table and address it with them personally when you get the chance, for example, at breaktime.

The Next Discussion

Make sure you give yourself enough time to write the next question on the board before the class finishes what they are doing.

If you are sitting with some students and the class goes quiet you know that they have almost finished with that discussion. In this case you are leaving things too late. There is nothing worse than a quiet class sitting there waiting for the next question as you write it up on the whiteboard.

If you have the next point ready and waiting for them to discuss, it looks and feels far more professional. It also really keeps the flow going and therefore a high level of attention.

With BTQs and roleplay this is especially important. Make sure you have enough time for preparation and do a good job of getting aims and objectives up on the whiteboard. You don't want to be rushing anything. While you are working on the white board you may be conscious that you have your back to the class for one or two minutes. Just remember, if you have already been active and interacted with your students you've done your job. You can't be everywhere all of the time.

Concept Checking Questions (CCQs)

Don't rush when explaining something. If you are setting up an activity and have your next activity ready up on the board make sure that everyone understands what they should be doing.

Be careful asking the class as a whole if everyone is clear on what you have just said. Though they will no doubt reply with a hearty "yes", the moment you start the activity some of your students will immediately dive for their dictionaries or ask their classmate explain it again for them.

If there are key words or grammar that you need to go over, double check that everyone is clear about it using CCQs. This is a more thorough way of making things clear and avoiding misunderstanding. They can be made in many ways; questions, demonstrations, examples, use of synonyms and antonyms and visual aids can all be used. Ask individual students rather than the class generally.

Example CCQ
Would you consider becoming a vegetarian? Why or why not? What are the advantages and disadvantages of being a vegetarian?

Teacher: "What is a vegetarian?"
Student: "Only eats vegetables?"
Teacher CCQ examples could be: "Can they eat anything else? Is a vegetarian a person or also an animal? Can they eat meat? Do they eat eggs and fish? Do they

drink milk? Do they wear leather? If someone answers "They don't eat meat" you can further this by asking "Will they eat meat in the future?"

Instruction Checking Questions (ICQs)

Before starting an activity you may want to check that they know exactly what they should be doing. This is particularly important before roleplay and group work. Remember, students are not mind readers and often some will say that they know what to do but have gotten the wrong end of the stick. Some ICQ's could be

"Are you working in pairs or threes? Are you working alone? Are you listening? Are you writing or talking?"

Correcting Student Errors

There are a number of ways to approach this. Always be mindful about how you go about correction as you certainly don't want to be damaging anyone's confidence.

Hot Correction

Firstly, you can choose to jump in and correct someone while they are speaking. This is known as 'hot correction'. Many of your students will make some kind of error nearly every sentence. In this sense the teacher must be selective about which areas need to be addressed. I personally use this

- Only if someone is making a really basic mistake.
- If someone is making a mistake you have repeatedly told them about.
- If they have asked you to do it. Maybe they have an English test waiting just around the corner or a professional has to work with some English speaking clients or colleagues in the near future.

The key is weighing out a balance between correction and allowing for fluency. Hot correction means you are actually stopping someone speaking. Not only that, you will also be interrupting a conversation between two or more people. If you are not careful you can damage someone's confidence, especially if they are a new or quiet student who is just getting off the ground.

Post Activity Correction Session (PACS)

An easy alternative to hot correction is to listen carefully to your class while they are doing an activity. If you hear any outstanding problems, make a note on the white board and address it with the whole class before you move on. PACS is an excellent way to work on an error as it may also be something that applies to more than one person. You can ask everyone to give their opinions and correct it instead of you. Also the focus is no longer on the individual who made the initial error. PACS also sends the message that their teacher is listening and cares about what they are doing.

Student to Student Correction
This is where students can help their classmate instead of the teacher doing it. If done correctly it can also be another excellent tool for sharpening your students listening skills and focusing on the task at hand. It is included in Appendix D with the quick fire activities as it can completely change the dynamics or a typical discussion question.

You need to set this up before the class starts talking either in pairs or threes. Anymore than that is intimidating for the speaker. Focus your students on listening to one aspect of speaking. I normally aim at listening to the tenses, especially the past tense as it is such a common area of inaccuracy.

Once again, it is really important that the speaker is not interrupted. Rather than stopping whoever is speaking, I get their partner to indicate that an error has just been made, for example, they can tap the table with their finger. If they are unable to correct themselves then their partner can do it. Student to student correction is therefore another excellent confidence builder.

One more great plus about this, is when students are listening, they are not looking at their dictionaries and planning what they will say when it's their turn. This means that they have to think spontaneously and move towards a more confident and fluent approach.

The Single Error Rule
To most students learning English feels like a sea of uncertainty filled with doubt and unanswered questions. Although they will quickly be building up their fluency they will also really need to know where they are going wrong. As a teacher this can also be a daunting task, especially if someone is making multiple errors in the same sentence. If you are teaching someone regularly the best course of action is to identify single targets that they can work on overnight. There are many positive gains from doing this. Setting a single target
- Transforms negative perceptions of learning language into feelings of clarity, vision and the obtainable.
- Sees swift improvement and therefore creates confidence.
- Aims at accuracy in that it focuses on a single problem.
- Harbours a workman like approach to learning.
- Allows the student to be mindful about the issue.
- If a student has other commitments such as a heavy workload outside the classroom, a single error target is something they can easily focus on without adding to their stress levels.

The Three Error Rule
I frequently get students coming up to me asking me what areas they need to look at in order to make a swift improvement. Again, this is normally when someone has their IELTS or TOEFL test coming up and they don't feel their level is up to scratch. If you are asked by one student, then pick out their outstanding errors. Make sure

you don't overload them with too many otherwise they may well become overwhelmed. Keep it down to three manageable tasks for them to focus on whenever they are speaking in English. Most of the time, the things that need to be ironed out will be repetitive mistakes that will really affect their score.

Giving Praise

Don't give praise too readily, but certainly don't forget to point it out when someone has done a good job. If you keep an eye on how much praise you give the class it will have that much more significance. What I'm saying is, that keeping a healthy balance between being too mean and too generous will always boost your students self achievement and therefore confidence. There are some key times to do this:

- When you are eliciting or asking questions and someone gives you the correct information look at them directly and say "Yes!" This powerful confirmation is the most positive thing you could possibly say to them and will also be heard by the rest of the class. This is an excellent confidence builder.
- When you are eliciting or asking questions and someone gives you the correct information you can also ask them to repeat what they have just said only much louder so the rest of the class can hear. If you do this you are setting what they say as a model, hence boosting their confidence. This is far better than the teacher repeating the answer often referred to as 'echoing'. Often if you echo a student they may think they have made a mistake.
- If you have a lower ability or quiet student who may be just starting, use someone in class who started off in a similar manner but has made significant progress as a model. Let your model student know you are referring to them.
- If you see someone showing definite signs of improvement then briefly acknowledge it while they are working being conscious of not interrupting them.
- If someone has clearly listened to and have worked on your recommendations from previous classes than let them know you have noticed.
- If you see some good teamwork going on let them know.
- If you see a good dynamic approach to discussion, argument or roleplay taking place where students are speaking freely, bring it to their attention.
- At the end of class, if they have worked hard or dealt with the topic well then give them a big well done before they leave. Topics like plants, religion, space and art can be particularly demanding.
- If there is anyone who has made significant progress, single them out before they go through the door and let others hear you do it.

Analysing Language

One very valuable thing you can do for your students is to go into more detail when going over a certain point. Write the target language clearly on the board and go through it step by step. Make sure you do it in this order:

Meaning: You can go into the definition of vocabulary or what is being expressed if you are looking at sentences, for example
"Can you answer the phone please?" is a simple and polite question.
"Can you please answer the phone?" implies that the phone has been ringing for sometime and they haven't answered yet.
Use CCQs to help you clarify things.
If I have time I like to ask the class if they know any synonyms for vocabulary or other ways to express the same meaning as it's so useful.

Pronunciation: I normally say the target language once and then get the students to repeat together a couple of times after. Try going round each student and listening to them in turn. They need to know if they are doing it right so I give them a simple 'yes' or 'no'. One word normally avoids too much embarrassment if it's not right. If they get a 'no' then give them another try after listening to you again.

On the white board, break down what you are trying to say. You may want to underline key points of pronunciation and write their phonetic equivalent underneath (see Appendix B: Using Phonetics).
You can also look at the strong sounds in a word such as 'comp*e*titor' or 'compet*i*tion'.

You can put something into context and analyse how it sounds changes when connected to other words. Connected speech is an important element in understanding spoken English and should be addressed regularly in these classes. To most students understanding the keys to native English speaking is a mystery that is yet to be unlocked. It is also why listening can be so difficult at times. Understanding this is what moves people away from standard text book English and is therefore something that I often highlight. It comes up in the topic 'Languages' (Part 2 and 'complete' version) and also in Appendix D: Quick Fire Activities.

Form: For vocabulary, go through whether it's an adverb, adjective, verb or noun. If it's a noun is it countable or uncountable, a personal or concept noun? For phrasal verbs is it separable or inseparable? You can look at different tenses of verbs. You can analyse sentence structure, in particular the most 'spoken' forms.

Another really useful thing you can do is asking your students to create new forms from your target language and put them into single groups, for example
Competition (concept noun)
Competitor (personal noun)
Competitive (adjective)
Compete (verb)

Quick Fire Activities

There are many additions you can make to your lesson to give it some more pep. These can be found in Appendix D. Sprinkle them in when need be, especially if your students are having an off day and need waking up. Remember that many in your class will be working long hours either at college or seven days a week in the office.

Dictionaries

Most students have access to some form of dictionary, whether it's on their phone, computer, tablet or even the good old traditional book with real pages. I personally recommend that every student has one for spoken English lessons and if they don't then they are sitting next to someone who has. They are not only useful if someone gets stuck when they are speaking but even more so when understanding the aims and objectives of various tasks.

There are instances though, when dictionaries can be overused so be mindful of these situations. Some students become reliant on their dictionary and will often have their head down, wasting precious talk time while focused on finding that certain word. If they are used during the Devil's Advocate and roleplay then they can be counterproductive to the exercise where the key focus is on fluency. If someone tries to find something on their dictionary in a group situation you may well see the others patiently waiting until their classmate has found what they wanted.

Be aware of the overuse of dictionaries. Encourage your class to try and think of other ways to complete a sentence or dialogue without reaching for it, for example, with the use of synonyms. Is what they are looking for really that essential?

Take a Back Seat

There are definitely times when it is ok to sit back and let them get on with it. This is especially so when they are doing the Devil's' Advocate or roleplay. Once they have started, take a break and enjoy listening in. You could also make notes on who attended your class, what the topic was and when, as this can prove to be very useful information at a later date.

Be on-call if someone needs some help. You can also casually move around the class and listen in and do a PACS later. It is ok to give a group some vocabulary that they can't think of as you walk past. Although you are giving them information, this keeps them in the flow of things rather than looking in their dictionaries.

7 The Lesson Plans

Topic 01 Age

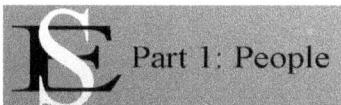 Part 1: People

Age

Vocabulary and useful stuff

Pregnant, labour, birth, delivery
Toddler, kid, boy & girl, child, childish
Teenager, puberty, acne, rebel
Young man, young adult, guy
In their 20's, early, mid 20's and late 20's
Mature, mid life, middle age, mid life crisis
Retire, pension, elder
Elderly, old, OAP
Death, bury, cremate, will, pass down, inherit

A: Hello to new students   5 minutes
Where is your hometown? What do you do here? Are you a student or do you have a job? Why are you learning English? Which country do you want to go to? Introduce yourself very briefly.

B: Brainstorm Timeline (*teacher's notes*)   10 minutes
Draw a horizontal line across the whiteboard broken into stages. Start at the beginning with students brainstorming for anything before the age of ten (take **10 minutes** for this). The timeline should be continuous throughout the lesson, with the last few discussions about old age. As you go through the lesson, brainstorm at the various key ages such as teenage or middle age.

C: Discussion

1: Describe your earliest childhood memory (past tense)   **10 minutes**
What age were you then? What happened?

2: How many kids do you want? (T6: Family)   **10 minutes**
Girls or boys? Why? Who should be the oldest?

3: What age does a boy become a man and a girl become a woman?
(T8: Dating) (*teacher's notes*)   **5 minutes**

4: Did you rebel when you were a teenager? (*teacher's notes*)   **10 minutes**
If not why not? In what ways did you rebel? Who against, your parents or teacher? In what ways did you rebel? Note: 'rebel' is a heteronym where the spelling stays the same but the meaning changes from verb and noun according to the stressed sound.

5: Open Discussion (*teacher's notes*)   **5 minutes**
What are the legal ages in China for a man and woman to get married?
Why are they different ages? Why can't a man get married earlier? Surely this is unfair?
(In China it is 20 for a woman and 22 for a man.)

Breaktime (5 minutes)

6: When is the best age to get married and why?   **10 minutes**
(T9: Marriage & Divorce)
Do you think it is different between a man and a woman? Why?

7: BTQ: What do you want to have achieved by the time you are 40?   **10 minutes**
(future tense)
Talk about career, which country you want to live in, your house, family, lifestyle and any special achievements for example, will have learnt to play an instrument, written a book or travelled to ten countries.

8: Open Discussion   **5 minutes**
What age do people retire in China?
Is it different for men and women? Why is there a difference? Why can't men retire early?
(In China it's normally 55 for women and 60 for men, though it will vary according to profession.)

9: Do you want to live beyond 100? Why or why not?   **10 minutes**

D: Devil's Advocate

A parent should not <u>spoil</u> their child.   **10 minutes**

E: Role Play

Retirement Home (*printables*)   **15 minutes**
<u>Person A:</u> You often work away from home. Your parents live in another city. You think your grandparents are too old to be left alone. Strongly encourage them to move to a nice old people's home.
Key words: The old people's home will be *safe, quiet, in the countryside, offer new hobbies, have nurses, soft food and nice music.*
<u>Person B:</u> Grandparent: You don't want to leave. You will feel lonely, miss your friends, routine and your family will forget about you. Refuse to leave. Be <u>stubborn.</u>

F: Filler Question
If you have a spare few minutes this is a good one to finish with.
What is the best age to be in life and why? I loved being a student as the partying and social life was so fantastic. Quick answer check.

G: Drilling the vocabulary and finish

Age
Additional Questions and Activities

1: What are the earliest lessons you learnt in life? **10 minutes**
How did you learn them and from who?

2: Describe where you grew up as a child? **10 minutes**
(T11 Houses and Apartments)
Which games did you play? Where was your house? In the city, countryside or <u>suburbs</u>?

3: Do parents influence their children too much? **10 minutes**
Give examples of where parents make decisions for their children. What would you do if your parents said no to something you wanted?

4: Mid Life: Present Tense **15 minutes**
<u>Person A:</u> Imagine you have reached middle age. Think about yourself at home, at work, doing a hobby. Describe to your friend what you are doing in the present tense, for example, "I am in my office. I have a great view of Shanghai. I am in my new suit" etc. Describe your lifestyle, job, country, city, kids.
<u>Person B:</u> Ask them questions about what they are describing.

5: Should people be made to retire? **10 minutes**
Should people be allowed to keep working if they wanted to?

6: Is it true to say you are only as old as you feel? **10 minutes**
Some people say "age is a state of mind." Do you agree? Why or why not?

7: Would you like to be <u>immortal</u>? Why or why not? **5 minutes**

8: Quick fire from the teacher asking individual students **5 minutes**
Would you like it if your girlfriend was older than you? Why or why not?
Would you like it if your boyfriend was younger than you? Why or why not?

<u>Devil's Advocate</u>

Parents influence their children too much in China. **10 minutes**
They should be allowed to make their own decisions and do what they want to do.

Retirement should be compulsory. **10 minutes**

Roleplay

Pocket Money 5 minutes
Person A: Child under 12. All your friends get more pocket money than you. Ask your parents for more money. Don't stop. Be persistent.
Parent B: Parents. No way! You think they already get enough. Give examples of how you already spoil them and why you shouldn't give them any more.

Child is watching too much TV 10 minutes
Person A: Parent. You think your child is watching too much TV and never doing their homework.
Person B: Child. Disagree with your parents. You do enough. You think your parents are being unfair.

You can also substitute this with:
Parents are not happy with son/daughters boyfriend/girlfriend or their choice of degree/major.

Unable to get a job 10 minutes
Person A: You are 45 and have been unemployed for six months. Go to a job interview for an office job. You must get this job.
Person B: Boss. You have lots of younger people who want the job. Why should you give the job to this person?

Fitness Evening for the Over 60's 20 minutes
(T5: Parts of the Body, *printables 4*)

Part 1 (10 minutes)
Person A: You own a gym and will be starting a new class every week for the over 60's. Interview an expert who can teach it.
Continually ask interview questions such as:
What experience do you have? Maybe they were an athlete, in the army, police or sports enthusiast. How long have you been an instructor?
Person B: You are a fitness expert. Talk about your previous experience and your ideas for creating a successful and interesting evening.
Talk about atmosphere, music, different exercises, maybe a theme evening, maybe some special food and drink. How will they benefit from your lessons?

Part 2 (10 minutes)
Write this up on the white board while they are doing Part 1. Keep the roles the same.

Person A: Boss: Some of your over 60's had to go to hospital after the first evening. Their family members complained that the exercises were too heavy. They asked for their money back. Angrily ask your new instructor what happened?
Person B: Instructor: make excuses to the boss. It wasn't your fault and you are not responsible.

Age
Printables

Person A:

You often work away from home. Your parents live in another city.

You think your grandparents are too old to be left alone. Strongly encourage them to move to a nice old people's home.

Key words: The old people's home will be *safe, be quiet, in the countryside, offer new hobbies, have nurses, soft food and nice music.*

Person B: Grandparent:

You don't want to leave. You will feel lonely, miss your friends and routine and your family will forget about you.

Refuse to leave.

Age
Teacher's Notes

Example of Age Timeline

boy/girl	rebel teenager		mid life			senior citizen old elderly	
0 10	20	30 40 50	60	70	80	100
birth toddler kid	legal ages puberty			retirement pension		kicked the bucket

3: What age does a boy become a man and a girl become a woman?
This is an especially interesting question in China, as it is the norm to keep saying someone is a girl or boy way into their late 20's and even 30's. Expect different answers from the students as there is no single right answer.

4: Did you rebel when you were a teenager?
Give examples of how you rebelled when you were a teenager. I grew my hair long, grew a beard and started listening to loud metal, punk and psychedelic music. I started drinking when I was 12 and smoking when I was 15. I had an electric guitar and a fuzz box. My Father hated it, especially all of my punk and metal friends. Obviously Chinese people are far more reserved, but they will still follow this easily into a discussion. It also gives them an insight how teenagers behave in our own culture.

The word 'rebel' is a heteronym. It has the same spelling but different pronunciation for different meanings. It can be a verb or noun depending on the stresses on the two vowels.

5: What are the legal ages in China for a man and woman to get married?
Trying to develop questions about legal ages in China is a no-no! There are no legal ages for smoking or drinking in China, though you have to be 18 to be able to drive and 17 to be in the army. Just telling them about western legal ages is enough, especially at 16 when you can have sex. Most Chinese students don't know about this.

7: Mid Life: Also talk about what a mid life crisis is all about in Western countries and what people do to overcome it. Don't put it into a discussion as most Chinese people don't experience this. If they are settled with a family and half decent job at the age of 40 then they are generally happy and contented.

Topic 02 Personality

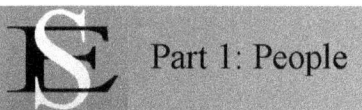

Part 1: People

Personality

Vocabulary and useful stuff

Character, characteristics, character traits
Cool, uncool
Good and bad tempered, irritable, snappy, short fused
Chilled out
Chatty
Extrovert, introvert
Overbearing
Tight fisted/tight (mean)
Hereditary, passed down
Refer to adverbs of degree in the printables of T4: Personal Appearance

A: Hello to new students   5 minutes
Where is your hometown? What do you do here? Are you a student or do you have a job? Why are you learning English? Which country do you want to go to? Introduce yourself very briefly.

B: Brainstorm   10 minutes
Split vocabulary up into positive and negative character traits. When you think you have enough, get the students to say what the opposite of each one is and add it to your list. Students often get character confused with feelings and emotions, so explain the differences.

C: Discussion

1: Describe your parent's positive and negative personality traits.   **10 minutes**

2: Now describe your own good and bad character traits.   **10 minutes**
Which come from your mother and which from your father?

3: Do you think you learn your character traits from your parents or they are hereditary?   **5 minutes**

4: Are you perfect? If there was one thing you would like to change about your character what would it be and why?   **10 minutes**

5: What are characteristics would your <u>ideal</u> husband or wife have and why?
(T9: Marriage & Divorce)   **5 minutes**

Breaktime (5 minutes)

6: Temper   **10 minutes**

Go through vocabulary before going into discussion:
Chilled out, relaxed, irritable, snappy, bad tempered, short fused Go through the difference between irritated and angry
Generally what kind of person are you? Good or bad tempered? Think of three things that irritate you. For example, someone smoking in the lift or spitting in the restaurant.

How do you calm down when you are angry or irritated?

7: Think of four ways you can use the word 'cool'.   **10 minutes**

Cool can describe someone's appearance, personality, something like a party or concert and is used in place of saying 'ok'. In Chinese people say 'xing xing xing' for example, when they are on the phone. We use 'cool' in the same way.
Use of the word 'uncool' for example, when people wear sunglasses on the subway.

8: Are you a caring person?   **10 minutes**

Describe the last time you helped someone. When was it and who was it for?

Do you care about the environment? Describe the last time you did something to help the environment.

9: Good and bad manners   **10 minutes**

Are you well mannered? Give examples of good and bad behaviour towards other people. Try and think of examples from both China and Western countries, for example, people talking very loudly on their mobile phones or pushing in front of a queue.

D: Role Play:

Shyness (T10: Parties)   **10 minutes**

<u>Person A:</u> You have been invited to a really cool party. Everyone will be there. Ask your friend to join you. No one likes going to a party alone.
<u>Person B:</u> You are really shy. You never go to parties. Think of as many reasons as you can not to go, for example, "*I am too busy, I don't like loud music, I don't like smoking, it will be too late and there may be drugs there*".

Overbearing Employee   **10 minutes**

<u>Person A:</u> Boss. You have had complaints that your new employee is irritating in the office. They are too chatty and loud. They don't take the job seriously. Tell them they must change their behaviour immediately.
<u>Person B:</u> Employee. Defend yourself.

E: Drilling the vocabulary and finish

Personality - Additional Questions and Activities

1: What makes a good boss?   **10 minutes**
    What makes a bad boss?

2: Job Compatibility   **10 minutes**
Choose one or two jobs and think of the ideal personality traits for each one. Would you be suited for these jobs and why?

2 Describe your personality when you were a teenager.   **10 minutes**
How have you changed? Compare it to how you are now.

3: What makes you different from other people?   **10 minutes**

4: Think of one thing that people don't know about your personality.   **10 minutes**

5: Popularity   **10 minutes**
Think of someone you know who is very popular. What makes them so popular?

6: Is it possible for opposites to attract?   **10 minutes**
Is it important for husband and wife to have the same personality traits or the same interests? Do you know any <u>couples</u> who are the <u>opposite</u>?

7: Determination (past tense)   **10 minutes**
Talk about a time where you never gave up and were successful. What <u>obstacles</u> did you have to overcome?

8: Bravery (past tense)   **10 minutes**
Hero, heroine, heroic, heroism, coward, cowardice, cowardly.
Talk about someone you know, heard about, saw in TV who was very brave. You can think about the Tangshan earthquake where there were many stories of bravery on the TV.

Roleplay

<u>Tight</u> with money   **10 minutes**
<u>Person A:</u> Its time to pay the bill in the restaurant. You forgot your wallet. Ask your friend if they can pay for you this time. Be persistent. They have to pay for you.
<u>Person B:</u> Your 'friend' never pays. They said they forgot their wallet last time and borrowed some money from you. They still haven't paid you back yet. Refuse to pay.
Note: You must state that both A and B are in the restaurant eating together.

Rude   **5 minutes**
Good to throw in at the end if you need to finish the class with lots of energy.
<u>Person A:</u> You are trying to study in the library. That person has been talking loudly on their phone for ten minutes. Ask them politely to be quiet.
<u>Person B:</u> Be as rude as possible. It is none of their business!

Topic 03
Feelings & Emotions

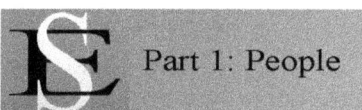 Part 1: People 03

Feelings and Emotions

Vocabulary and useful stuff (*teacher's notes*)
Boring, bored
Exciting and excited
Confusing and confused
Interesting and interested – See Appendix C: Common Student Errors
Hysterical laughter, crying with laughter, laughing until my sides hurt, laughing fit, LOL
Turn nouns into adjectives e.g. anxiety/anxious
Refer to adverbs of degree in the printables of T4: Personal Appearance

A: Hello to new students   5 minutes
Where is your hometown? What do you do here? Are you a student or do you have a job? Why are you learning English? Which country do you want to go to? Introduce yourself very briefly.

B: Brainstorm   10 minutes
Similar to Topic 02: Personality; you can put anything the students say into two columns, one for positive and the other for negative emotions. Once you have gone around the class and built up a reasonable list, you can ask them what the opposite of each word is, for example, 'bored' and 'interested'. People normally think in terms of adjectives for this topic, so make clear the differences between these and uncountable nouns, for example, 'anger' and 'angry'.

C: Discussion

1: Describe the happiest moment in your life. (past tense)   **10 minutes**

2: Why are you proud of your country?   **5 minutes**

3: BTQ: **Excitement** (past and future tenses)   **10 minutes**
Describe the most exciting time you can remember in your life. When was it? Who were you with and what happened?
Describe something exciting you hope to do in the future that will be exciting.

4: Humour (past tense)   **10 minutes**
Vocab: *Hysterical laughter, crying with laughter, laughing until my sides hurt, laughing fit, LOL*

What was the funniest thing that happened to you? Tell a funny story.
What was the funniest thing that you saw on TV?

A challenge: Tell a joke or try and make your friend laugh   **5 minutes**

Breaktime (5 minutes)

5: Depression (*teacher's notes*)   **10 minutes**
Vocab: Prozac, bi-polar
What is depression? What causes depression? What can you do to overcome depression?
Answer Check

6: Fear and phobias   **10 minutes**
Think of two things that you are afraid of. Why are you afraid of them? Teacher should give some examples of some phobias such as claustrophobia, arachnophobia.
Answer Check

7: Think of four questions that a psychiatrist may ask their patient.   **10 minutes**
(*There are some examples in the teacher's notes*) Also called a 'shrink' in the US.
Answer Check: Make sure you write the answers on the white board. You will need them for the role play later.

8: Jealousy, Envy and Admiration   **5 minutes**
What are the differences?
Briefly talk about someone who you admire.
Answer Check

9: Talk about something embarrassing that happened to you. (past tense) **10 minutes**

D: Role Play

Visit a Psychiatrist (*printables 1*)   **15 minutes**
Encourage your students to use the material from Q7 which should already be on the white board.
This will easily run through till the end of class. Use the flash cards in the printables section. Give students a few minutes to read and understand them using dictionaries.

Person A: Take one of the flash cards. This is your problem. Visit a psychiatrist to help you.
Person B: You are the psychiatrist. Ask your patient questions about their problem. Find out the cause of the problem and give advice to your patient. You can also try and recommend some medication.

After 10 minutes swap roles and give the other student one of the flash cards so that the patient becomes the psychiatrist and visa versa.

E: Drilling the vocabulary and finish

Feeling and Emotions
Additional Questions and Activities

1: Anxiety (past tense)   **10 minutes**
Anxious, nervous, worried, panic/anxiety attacks
When do you get nervous? Talk about a time you remember when you got really nervous.
When was it and what were you doing? How did you feel at the time?

2: BTQ Stress   **10 minutes**
What are the most stressful times in life? What are the most stressful jobs and why?
When do you feel stress in daily life?
What are your personal ways to deal with stress?
Thinks of four ways stress affects your body.

3: Love   **10 minutes**
What is the difference between loving someone and being in love?
What are the symptoms of being in love?
Think of and talk about three things you love, for example, *food, family, best friend, hobby, music.*

4: Sense of Achievement (past tense)   **10 minutes**
What has been the thing that has brought you the most satisfaction or the greatest feeling of achievement in your life? Why?

Roleplay

Fear of flying   **10 minutes**
Person A: You are going abroad today with your grandparents. The plane will be taking off shortly.
Person B: Grandparent: You have never flown before and are really afraid to get on the plane. Think of as many reasons not to go as you can.
Person A: Persuade your grandparents to go. Your bags are already on the plane.

Negotiating a pay rise (*printables 2*)   **15 minutes**
Spend five minutes explaining this, going over each role separately.
Try and get people into groups of three for this. If you are only able to put your class into pairs, get them to play person A and person C.
An excellent thing to do here is to get them to interrupt each other. Write the word 'interrupt' on the white board and ask them what it means. As they answer, start talking to them again before they finish.

Person A: Manager. You are irritated and slightly annoyed by this employee.
You don't like this employee. They are often late.
They are often on their mobile phone for personal calls.
They don't complete tasks on time.

You don't like that this employee is the other managers relative. You think they get special treatment and should be treated equally like all the other staff.

Person B: Manager. You are caring and sympathetic to your employee.
This employee is your relative. You know the pressures they have in their life.
However, recently their standards of work have dropped.
They are often late.
They are often on their mobile phone for personal calls.
They don't complete tasks on time.

Think of ways to help your employee.

Person C: Employee. You are depressed and stressed out. Recently you have had some great pressure in your life. Your boss A is giving you too much work.
The company moved to a new office which is far away from your apartment.
However, your husband/wife has said that you need to be earning more money.
You have been at the company for three years. All other staff have had a pay increase except you.

Your Boss B will help you. He is one of your relatives. Negotiate for a pay increase.

Anger: Pizza delivery driver **15 minutes**

Part 1 (10 minutes)
Person A: You ordered a pizza to be delivered to your apartment over two hours ago. You already phoned the shop, but it has still not arrived. Phone again and ask what has happened. Be angry.
Person B: You work in the restaurant. Answer the phone and make excuses why the pizza has still not been delivered.

Part 2 (5 minutes)
Person A: Finally after three hours the driver has arrived with your pizza. It is cold and you have already eaten now. Refuse to pay. Be angry.
Person B: Delivery driver. Make excuses as to why you are late. They must pay. Your boss will be angry if they don't.

In the second part, make sure the same student stays as Person A

Feelings and Emotions
Printables 1: Psychiatrist - Patient Flash Cards

I seem to get angry very easily.
I often upset my friends and get into arguments in public places.

Help me doctor

I am afraid of dogs – 'cynophobia'

Help me doctor

I can't stop cleaning and tidying. I have to clean the apartment every day. It drives my wife/husband crazy. I make them change their clothes twice a day – 'ataxophobia' – fear of untidiness

Help me doctor

My apartment has no mirrors. I hate mirrors. I am afraid of seeing my reflection even in a shop window. I can't drive or use a taxi as they have mirrors – 'eisoptrophobia' - fear of seeing yourself in a mirror

Help me doctor

I can't stop stealing things. So far I only steal small things. I also steal from shops - 'kleptomania' – cant stop stealing

Help me doctor

I eat a lot when I get home, especially when I am watching TV. Sometimes I eat without thinking. I can't stop. I am getting fat.
Comfort eating / Compulsive eating

Help me doctor

I am a shopaholic. I have to go shopping 3 or 4 times a week and always at the weekends. I am seriously in debt to 6 credit card companies.

Help me doctor

I don't trust my wife/husband anymore. This happened before and I got divorced – 'paranoia'

Help me doctor

I often feel very nervous. Sometimes I can't breathe. Sometimes I feel sick – 'anxiety' or 'panic attack'

Help me doctor

I am scared of my mother-in-law. I am always very nervous if we have a family meeting – 'pentheraphobia'

Help me doctor

I am depressed. I have been depressed for a long time. I have tried many things but nothing has been successful.

Help me doctor

I am unpopular and often I feel very lonely.

I am so unhappy.

Help me doctor

I hate eating. If I eat it is very occasionally. I have lost a lot of weight. My family are worried about me – 'anorexia'

Help me doctor

I am an alcoholic. I drink every night. My boss has noticed and warned me. I often smell of alcohol. I can't stop.

Help me doctor

I am afraid of flying. It drives my family crazy when we go on holiday. 'aviophobia'

Help me doctor

I am afraid of getting married. I haven't told my girlfriend/boyfriend yet. Their parents and friends are asking why I haven't asked her to marry me yet – 'gamophobia'

Help me doctor

I am afraid of the dark. I have to sleep with the lights on.
'nyctophobia'

Help me doctor

I am very shy and quiet. Especially around members of the opposite sex. I have never had a girlfriend/boyfriend.

Help me doctor

I am afraid of being alone. I am always on the phone. If my husband/wife goes out I always go with them – 'autophobia'

Help me doctor

Printables 2: Negotiating a pay rise (Additional Questions & Activities)

A: Manager
You are irritated/slightly annoyed by this employee

You don't like this employee.
They are often late. They are often on their mobile phone for personal calls.
They don't complete tasks on time.
You don't like that this employee is the other managers relative. You think they get special treatment and should be treated equally like all the other staff.

B: Manager
You are caring and sympathetic to your employee

This employee is your relative. You know the pressures they have in their life.
However, recently their standards of work have dropped.
They are often late. They are often on their mobile phone for personal calls.
They don't complete tasks on time.
Think of ways to help your employee.

C: Employee
You are depressed and stressed out

Recently you have had some great pressure in your life.
Your boss A is giving you too much work.
The company moved to a new office which is far away from your apartment.
However, your husband/wife has said that you need to be earning more money.
You have been at the company for three years. All the other staff have had a pay increase except you.

Your Boss B will help you. He is one of your relatives.
Negotiate for a pay increase.

Feelings and Emotions
Teacher's Notes

Feelings and Emotions Vocab' List:

Negative and forceful: Anger, Annoyance, Contempt, Disgust, Irritation

Negative and not in control: Anxiety, Embarrassment, Fear, Helplessness, Lonely, Powerlessness, Worry

Negative thoughts: Doubt, Envy, Frustration, Guilt, Shame

Negative and passive: Boredom, Despair, Disappointment, Hurt, Sadness

Agitation: Stress, Shock, Tension

Positive and lively: Amusement, Delight, Elation, Excitement, Happiness, Joy, Pleasure

Caring: Affection, Empathy, Friendliness, Love

Positive thoughts: Courage, Hope, Pride, Satisfaction, Trust

Quiet positive: Calm, Content, Relaxed, Relieved, Serene

Reactive: Interest, Politeness, Surprised

5: Depression   15 minutes
This normally runs longer than you think. Most Chinese students don't really know what depression is all about. Actually you won't hear about anyone in China who suffers from it. People normally keep their problems quiet.
Let them try and answer the question for a few minutes until they run out of steam, then plough in with some extra teacher talk time, where if you can, give a few examples of someone you met suffering from it, the cause and symptoms. You will find that your students will be very interested in what you have to say.
Vocab: 'Prozac' and 'bi-polar' need explaining. I also include the meaning of the term 'baggage' here, as this can also contribute to depression.

6: Think of four questions that a psychiatrist may ask their patient.
How long have you been feeling like this? When did it start? Talk about your dreams?
When you look at this picture what do you see?
Do you think your parents may have any influence on you?
Did anything important happen to you in your childhood that may be the cause?
How does it affect you in daily life? When do you notice your problem?

Topic 04: Personal Appearance

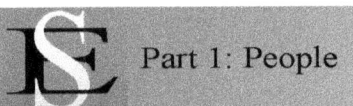 Part 1: People

Personal Appearance

Vocabulary and useful stuff

Figure, shape, build, hour-glass figure
Slim, slender, skinny, thin, anorexic
Underweight
Overweight, fat, obese, comfort eating
White lie
Athletic, toned
Hair: Blonde, brunette, grey/silver/white/pink rinse, ginger, bald, wig, toupee, dyed, 'comb over'
A turn-on, turn-off, 'man-eater', 'lady-killer'
Cosmetics, make-up
Cool, uncool

A: Hello to new students   5 minutes
Where is your hometown? What do you do here? Are you a student or do you have a job? Why are you learning English? Which country do you want to go to? Introduce yourself very briefly.

B: Adverbs of Degree: (*printables 1*)   10 minutes
Use the adverbs of degree found in the printables. Hand a few out to each student. Also give them some Blue Tack, board magnets or tape. They should leave their seats and stick them on the wall or white board in order of strength. It also works if you have enough space to arrange them on the floor. Ask individual students if they agree with the order and they think it is correct. They can change anything they like.

C: Discussion

1: Think of five ways to stay looking young and healthy.   10 minutes
Answer Check

2: Obesity   10 minutes
These days in the West it is very common to see people who are overweight. Why do so many people become too heavy? How have our lifestyles changed in recent years for this to happen? (*comfort eating*) Why do people comfort eat?

3: Anorexia and Bulimia (*teacher's notes*)   10 minutes
Many people also under eat. Some people suffer from anorexia or bulimia. Describe both and ask why people may suffer from these disorders.

You could use Karen Carpenter as an example for anorexia as most Chinese people know her, though you may have to sing a few songs to jog their memory.

4: What things do you find attractive in the opposite sex?   **10 minutes**
A turn on, a turn off
This can include someone's personality aswell as how someone looks, for example, you might think that someone's smile can be really attractive especially if they have a great sense of humour.

Breaktime (5 minutes)

5: Give a compliment (*teacher's notes*)   **5 minutes**
Also 'pay' a compliment. In pairs get each student to pay each other a compliment.

6: Men and Long Hair   **5 minutes**
Guys: Would you like to grow your hair long? Why or why not?
Girls: Would you like it if your boyfriend had long hair? Why or why not?

D: Devil's Advocate

People dress far too casually at work these days with t-shirts, jeans and sports shoes.
Staff should take pride in their company and therefore their appearance.
    10 minutes

E: Role Play:

Image consultant (*teacher's notes*) (*printables 2*)   **10 minutes**
Person A: You are 50 years old. You are still not married and have never had a girlfriend or boyfriend. You have a date this weekend. It's really important. Go and visit an <u>image consultant</u> and ask for advice on changing your appearance.

Person B: Image consultant: Give advice on how this person can change the way they look. Think about hair style, clothes, shoes, accessories and also maybe there is something with their behaviour that needs changing.

Holiday with the Grandparents (*teacher's notes*) (*printables 3*)   **10 minutes**
Person A: You will be going on holiday for two weeks with your grandparent next week. Give them advice on improving their appearance. They always wear the same <u>dull</u> brown old clothes. Recommend some bright new, younger looking clothes. Maybe they could change their hair.
Person B: Grandparent. Strongly disagree and be <u>stubborn</u>. You like your clothes; they are familiar and comfortable. Refuse to change the way you look.

You can also use the handout on fashion design found in the printables section of T14: Clothes & Fashion

Cosmetics   **20 minutes**
Think of five types of cosmetic product
Ask the students and very quickly write a few on the board, such as
Lipstick, eye liner, foundation, perfume, cologne and aftershave.

Cosmetic Sales Part 1: (*printables 4*)   **(10 minutes)**
Put people into groups of 3 or 4. One person should be the salesperson.
<u>Person A:</u> Salesperson: Promote a new beauty product in a supermarket. Try and sell it to some customers. Why will it make them <u>irresistible</u> to the <u>opposite sex</u>? Why is this product so great? How do they use it?

<u>Person B and C:</u> Customers: You are unsure about buying this product. Continually ask questions about it, for example, Is it tested on animals? Which ones and how? How long should I use it for? What is it made of?

Part 2:   **(10 minutes)**
Write this part up on the white board while they are doing Part 1.
<u>Person B and C:</u> Customers: You bought that product and after only one day your skin <u>came out</u> in a bad <u>rash</u>. You had to go to hospital and missed work. Your boss is angry with you. You look terrible. Return to the shop and demand your money back and the hospital fee. Be persistent.

<u>Person A:</u> Salesperson. It is not your fault. Think of an excuse not to pay back the money. Blame the customer.

F: <u>Drilling the vocabulary and finish</u>

Personal Appearance
Additional Questions and Activities

1: Describe the most attractive person you ever met.   **10 minutes**
Why were they so attractive? Remember personality also has a strong influence how someone looks.

2: If you looked like 007 or Angelina Jolie would you like to be a <u>cat-walk</u> model?
Why or why not? (T14: Clothes & Fashion)   **5 minutes**

3: Quick fire from the teacher asking individual students   **5 minutes**
Would you like it if your boyfriend was shorter than you? Why or why not?
Would you mind if your girlfriend was taller than you? Why or why not?
Would you like it if your girlfriend/boyfriend had an <u>athletic</u> build?

4: Tattoos and Piercings   **10 minutes**
Think of six places on the body that people get pierced.
Would you get a tattoo or piercing? Why or why not? If yes, where would it be?

5: Beards and Moustaches   **10 minutes**
Guys: Would you like to grow a beard or moustache? Why or why not?
Girls: Would you like it if your boyfriend had a beard or moustache? Why or why not?

6: What is your opinion of high heeled shoes? (T14: Clothes & Fashion)   **10 minutes**
How do they affect the legs and feet?
Girls: Do you wear them? Why or why not? How often? How long for? How high?
Men: Do you prefer a woman to wear high heels? Why or why not?

7: Hair styles   **10 minutes**
1: Think of six hair colours and six styles. There's a lot of vocabulary so limit it.
2: How could your partner improve their hairstyle?
Brunette, brown, auburn, ginger, red head, blonde, black
Grey, silver, white, a pink rinse, dye, highlights, peroxide
Extensions, wig, bald, toupee, a 'comb over' (a noticeably Chinese style. Draw this on the board. Describe how a comb over can lift up in the wind), *centre parting, side parting*
A number one, Long, short, a bob, medium
Dreads, straight, curly, perm, fringe
Mohawk

8: Cosmetic Surgery (*T5: Parts of the Body, printables 2*)   **15 minutes**
Vocab: *Liposuction, bone shave, facelift, eye, nose and boob job.*
Think of four types of cosmetic surgery. What is your opinion about it?
Look at the pictures. Describe what these famous people have had done. Do you think they look better or worse? Why?

9: Think of four ways you can use the word 'cool'.   **10 minutes**
(T2: Personality)
Cool can describe someone's appearance, personality, something like a party or concert and is used in place of saying 'ok'. In Chinese people say 'xing xing xing", for example, when they are on the phone. We use 'cool' in the same way.
Use of the word 'uncool', for example, when people wear sunglasses on the subway.

10: Think or five ways to lose weight.   **10 minutes**
Mention the Atkins diet, liposuction and getting your teeth wired.

Devil's Advocate
                                                                               15 minutes
If you are lucky enough to have an equal number of girls and guys then use these two separate discussions to really get them arguing.

Guys: Women spend far too long on their appearance. Women should look natural in order to look good. Girls disagree.

Girls: Men are generally lazy and should spend more time on their appearance.
Guys disagree

Roleplay

Weight loss pills (*printables 5*)   **15 minutes**
Can be in pairs or small groups. Make one person the salesperson.

Part 1:   (10 minutes)
Person A: Salesperson. Your company has some new weight loss pills. They work very well. Sell them to some customers in a supermarket.
When should they be taken? How many? How much weight will they lose?
Person B: Customers. You do think you are overweight. Ask the salesperson about these tablets. Do they have any side effects? How are they tested? Do they really work? How should I take them?

Part 2:   (5 minutes)
Person B: Customer. Return to the supermarket. Those pills had some serious side effects. You couldn't sleep, you couldn't eat anything and you feel really depressed. Demand your money back.
Person A: Refuse to return the money. They have clearly lost weight.

Image consultant alternative (*teacher's notes*)   **10 minutes**
You can use the handout on fashion design in the printables of T14 Clothes & Fashion.
Person A: You are going on a business trip to Shanghai for the weekend. It's really important. Ask a consultant to help you with formal, informal clothing, daytime and evening clothing.
Person B: Image consultant: Give advice on how this person can change the way they look. Think about hair style, clothes, shoes, accessories and also maybe there is something with their behaviour that need changing.

Personal Appearance
Printables 1

Adverbs of Degree

almost absolutely awfully
badly barely
completely
decidedly deeply
enough enormously
entirely extremely
fairly far fully
greatly
hardly highly hugely
incredibly indeed intensely
just least less little lots
massively most much
nearly
perfectly positively practically pretty purely
quite
rather really
seriously scarcely simply so somewhat strongly
terribly thoroughly too totally
utterly
very virtually well

Print these off and hand a few out to each student. Also give them some Blue Tack, board magnets or tape. They should then stick them on the wall in order of strength. It also works if you have enough space to arrange them on the floor. Ask your students if they agree with the order and they think it is correct. They can change anything they like.

enormously

hugely

extremely

terribly

seriously

greatly

totally

completely

really

almost

very

nearly

kinda

fairly

quite

a bit

barely

scarcely

hardly

Printables 2

Image consultant

Person A:

You are 50 years old. You are still not married and have never had a girlfriend or boyfriend.

You have a date this weekend. It's really important.

Go and visit an <u>image consultant</u> and ask for advice on changing your appearance.

Person B: Image consultant

Give advice on how this person can change the way they look.

Think about hair style, clothes, shoes and <u>accessories</u>.

Also maybe there is something with their behaviour that needs changing.

Printables 3

Holiday with the Grandparents

Person A:

You will be going on holiday for two weeks with your grandparent next week.

Give them advice on improving their appearance.

They always wear the same <u>dull</u> brown old clothes.

Recommend some bright new, younger looking clothes. Maybe they could change their hair.

Person B: Grandparent

Strongly disagree and be stubborn.

You like your clothes; they are familiar and comfortable.

Refuse to change the way you look.

Printables 4

Cosmetic Sales Part 1:

Person A:

You Salesperson: Promote a new beauty product in a supermarket. Try and sell it to some customers. Why will it make them <u>irresistible</u> to the <u>opposite sex</u>?

Why is this product so great?

How do they use it?

Person B and C: Customers

You are unsure about buying this product.

Continually ask questions about it for example, Is it tested on animals? Which ones and how?

How long should I use it for?

What is it made of?

Printables 5

Weight Loss Pills:

Person A: Salesperson

Your company has some new weight loss pills. They work very well.

Sell them to some customers in a supermarket.

When should they be taken? How many? How much weight will they lose?

Person B: Customers

You do think you are overweight.

Ask the salesperson about these tablets.
Do they have any side effects? How are they tested? Do they really work?
How should I take them?

Personal Appearance
Teacher's Notes

It's very easy for this topic to cross over with T5: Parts of the Body so be careful if you are teaching these topics on sequence or within a short period of time.

4: Anorexia and Bulimia
<u>Anorexia</u> is where someone may have general loss of appetite or no interest in food. Not to be confused with Anorexia Nervosa.
<u>Anorexia Nervosa</u> is where people are afraid of becoming overweight. They may deliberately try and lose weight.
<u>Bulimia Nervosa</u> is where someone experiences regular bouts of serious overeating, which are always followed by a feeling of guilt and them extreme reactions such as crash dieting, doing lots of exercise, or purging/being sick.

6: Give a compliment
During break write this up on the board. Underlined words should be emphasised in the sentence:

"<u>Wow</u>, you look <u>great</u> today! Where <u>did</u> you get that shirt/dress from?" (also hair done/ hair cut). Drill it a few times with the students including the word 'Wow' by itself. Get them to do it with conviction, including a look of 'Wow' in their faces. Show them how we use our foreheads to help communicate. They should copy your example.

Also go through a typical 'playing it down' answer such as 'Oh it's nothing special'.

Role Play:
Image Consultant and Holiday with the Grandparents
You can write a few key words on the board while they are doing their Devil's Advocate. You can elicit it, but it's generally best for them to just get on with it and keep up the rhythm of the class.
<u>Pattern</u>, <u>stripes</u>, <u>spots</u>, material, man made, natural, sexy, <u>low cut</u>, formal, casual, colours, warm, seasonal, women's, men's, sports, matching, younger, energetic.
<u>Accessories</u>: *(elicit this) bags, hats, belts, gloves, scarf, tie.*

Topic 05: Parts of the Body

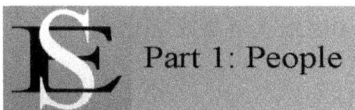 Part 1: People

05

Parts of the Body

Vocabulary and useful stuff

Anatomy, organs, muscles, bones, skeleton
Tattoo, piercing
Eyes: lids, lashes, brow, (wink, blink, stare, glare)
Forehead, frown
Nose: nostrils, bridge
Shoulders, elbow, wrist, forearm
Chest, waist
Thigh, knee, ankle
Cosmetic surgery/plastic surgery, liposuction, face-lift, bone shave (usually on the either side of the jaw), nose-job

A: Hello to new students   5 minutes
Where is your hometown? What do you do here? Are you a student or do you have a job? Why are you learning English? Which country do you want to go to? Introduce yourself very briefly.

B: Hangman or Brainstorm   10 minutes
Playing hangman to elicit vocabulary can be effective here using words like 'anatomy' or 'skeleton'. If you have a big class then it's best to revert to generally brainstorming on the topic instead.
The list of parts of the body is of course endless. You need to create a simple list of vocabulary they can use without overwhelming them.
1 A list of body parts from head to foot. They will already know the basics such as 'head, eyes, ears, arms, legs' etc so go into more detail, for example, parts of the eye.
2 A list of organs, a few bones and muscles.

C: Discussion

1: Are you 100% healthy?   5 minutes
When are you unhealthy in life and how does it affect the different parts of your body?

2: Would you give blood? Why or why not?
   Would you donate organs after you die? Why or why not?   10 minutes

3: The Brain   15 minutes
Think of three things you know about the brain:
- The brain is 75% water

- Bilingual brains. Children who learn two languages before the age of five alter their brain structure forever.
- When you are asleep, if you are snoring you are not dreaming.

Which is the dominant side of your brain? (*printables 1*)   (10 minutes)

The right hand side is considered to be the creative side: dreamers, good at art and sport, like rock music, prefer learning visually with examples, like fiction, enjoy story telling, are cat lovers.

The left hand side is considered to be the logical, thinking side: good at maths, like non-fiction, logical, good memory, prefer structure in their lives, like dogs, well organised.

5: Why do people smoke?   **15 minutes**

1: Surely it is totally crazy! Do you think smoking is a good or bad thing? How does it affect your health? Would you marry a smoker?

2: What advice could you give someone who wanted to stop smoking?

3: Which of the following would be the best way to reduce smoking? What would the advantages or advantages in each case?

- Treble the price of cigarettes
- Make smoking illegal
- Launch a public health campaign
- Limit smoking to very specific areas
- Something else

Breaktime (5 minutes)

6: What is your opinion of people who have cosmetic surgery?   **15 minutes**
(*printables 2*)

Think of five different types of cosmetic surgery, for example, in South Korea it is really popular for people to have their eyes changed.

What is your opinion of famous and rich people who have cosmetic surgery?
Think of someone who has had bad cosmetic surgery.

Hand out the photos of famous people who have had cosmetic surgery. When students have finished with one, they can pass them on to their neighbour.
1: Do they look better or worse after their cosmetic surgery?
2: Describe the changes that they have had.

D: Devil's Advocate

Alcohol and McDonalds can be advertised. Cigarette companies should be allowed to advertise aswell. **10 minutes**

E: Role Play:

Check up at the doctors (*printables 3*) **10 minutes**

<u>Person A:</u> Go for a <u>check up</u> at the doctors. You are a workaholic, working seven days a week under a lot of pressure. You don't eat properly and neglect your family. Recently you have had some bad chest and stomach pains.
<u>Person B:</u> Doctor. This person will have some serious health problems if they are not careful. Recommend immediate changes in lifestyle; exercise, relaxation, better food. What parts of their body are at risk?
<u>Person A:</u> : Disagree with the doctor. It is impossible to change.

Fitness Evening for the Over 60's (*printables 4*) **20 minutes**
Part 1 (10 minutes)

<u>Person A:</u> You own a gym and will be starting a new class every week for the <u>over 60's</u>. Interview an expert who can teach it.
Continually ask interview questions such as:
What experience do you have? Maybe they were an athlete, in the army, police or sports enthusiast. How long have you been an instructor?
<u>Person B:</u> You are a fitness expert. Talk about your previous experience and your ideas for creating a successful and interesting evening.
Talk about atmosphere, music, different exercises, maybe a theme evening, maybe some special food and drink. How will they benefit from your lessons?

Part 2 (10 minutes)
Write this up on the white board while they are doing Part 1. Keep the roles the same.

<u>Person A:</u> Boss: Some of your over 60's had to go to hospital after the first evening. Their family members complained that the exercises were too heavy. They asked for their money back. Angrily ask your new instructor what happened?
<u>Person B:</u> Instructor: make excuses to the boss. It wasn't your fault and you are not responsible.

F: Drilling the vocabulary and finish

Parts of the Body
Additional Questions and Activities

1: How does using your computer for too long affect different parts of your body?
10 minutes
How long do you spend on your computer every week/month? If you continue how will your body have changed in ten years time?

2: Teeth **10 minutes**
Front, back, upper, lower, incisors, wisdom teeth.
How often do you brush your teeth?
How often do you change your toothbrush?
When was the last time you went to the dentist? What for?
How often you go for a check up?
Do you have perfect teeth?
Would you like to be a dentist? Why or why not?

3: Think of six common places in the body that people have pierced? **5 minutes**
Would you like to have a piercing or your partner to have one? Why or why not?

4: Body language **15 minutes**
Think of 4 ways we use our eyes to communicate
Think of 4 ways we use our forehead to communicate
Think of 4 ways we use our body to communicate
Think of 8 ways we use our hands to communicate
Which are rude? Which can be important?

Devil's Advocate

It doesn't matter what a person looks like. It is the personality that is the most important when looking for a girlfriend or boyfriend. **10 minutes**

Roleplay

Check up at the doctors (*printables 3*) **10 minutes**

Person A: Go for a check up at the doctors. You are a serious couch potato. You don't have a job and haven't worked for a long time. You are unhappy and eat a lot in the afternoons and evenings while watching TV.
You are now overweight and have some serious stomach and heart pains.
Person B: Doctor. This person will have some serious health problems if they are not careful. Recommend immediate changes in lifestyle; exercise, relaxation, better food. What parts of their body are at risk?
Person A: Disagree with the doctor. It is impossible to change.

Cigarette Company   **30 minutes**

Part 1: (optional)   (10 minutes)
<u>Person A:</u> Government representative. Announce that from now on cigarette companies will be allowed to advertise in China.
<u>Person B:</u> CCTV interviewer. Continually ask follow up questions? Why is this being allowed? Where will they be allowed to advertise? Won't this affect people's health?

Part 2   (10 minutes)
Split your class into even groups.
Each group owns a cigarette company. They have produced a new brand of cigarette.
Think of the <u>target market</u> who will buy the product.
Think of the name of your cigarettes. Write down your ideas.

Part 3   (10 minutes)
Place your groups together, so you have two groups working together, Group A and B.
One group will become the customers.
<u>Group A:</u> Your company has a new brand of cigarettes. Give them to people to sample outside a supermarket.
<u>Group B:</u> Customers. You hate cigarettes and what they do to people. You think they are disgusting. Strongly voice your disapproval to these people. Be angry.

Parts of the Body
Printables 1

The Brain:

Which is side of your brain is dominant?

Right Side:
Is said to be the creative side: dreamers, good at art and sport, like rock music, prefer learning visually with examples, like <u>fiction</u>, enjoy story telling and are cat lovers.

Left Side:
Is said to be the logical, thinking side: good at maths, like <u>non-fiction,</u> logical, good memory, prefer structure in their lives, like dogs and well organised.

Cosmetic Surgery – Printables 2

Mickey Rourke before:

Mickey Rourke after

Nicole Kidman before:

Nicole Kidman after:

Meg Ryan before:

Meg Ryan after:

Angelababy before:

Angelababy after:

Sylvester Stallone before:

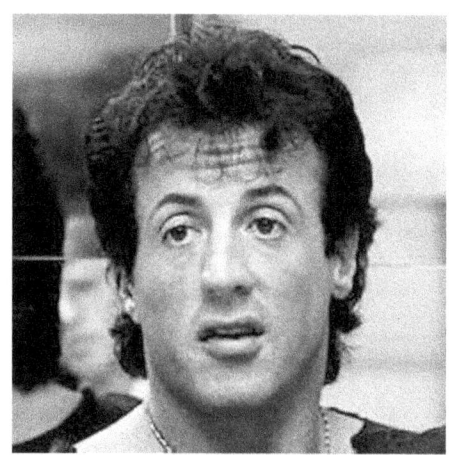

Sylvester Stallone after:

Li Bing Bing: before and after

Printables 3: Roleplay – A Check up at the doctors

Person A: Go for a **check up** at the doctors.

You are a workaholic, working seven days a week under a lot of pressure. You don't eat properly and neglect your family. Recently you have had some bad chest and stomach pains.

Disagree with the doctor. It is impossible to change.

Alternative

Person A: Go for a check up at the doctors.

You are a serious <u>couch potato</u>. You don't have a job and haven't worked for a long time. You are unhappy and eat a lot in the afternoons and evenings while watching TV.

You are now overweight and have some serious stomach and heart pains.

Disagree with the doctor. It is impossible to change.

Person B: Doctor.

This person will have some serious health problems if they are not careful.

Recommend immediate changes in lifestyle; exercise, relaxation, better food. Which parts of their body are at risk?

Printables 4: Fitness Evening for the Over 60's: Part 1

Person A: **You own a gym**
and will be starting a new class every week for the <u>over 60's</u>. Interview an expert who can teach it.

Continually ask interview questions such as:
What experience do you have? Maybe they were an athlete, in the army, police or sports enthusiast. How long have you been an instructor?

Person B: You are a fitness expert.

Talk about your previous experience and your ideas for creating a successful and interesting evening.

Talk about atmosphere, music, different exercises, maybe a theme evening, maybe some special food and drink.

How will they benefit from your lessons?

Topic 06 Family

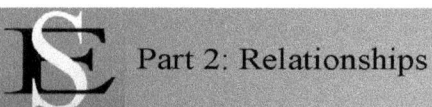 Part 2: Relationships 06

Family

Vocabulary and useful stuff

Great great grandmother
Ancestors
Mum (UK), mom (US)
Dad (UK), pa (US)
Niece: 'daughter of a person's brother or sister'
Cousin: 'the son or daughter of an uncle or aunt'
Nephew: 'a son of one's brother or sister'.
Step Son: 'a son of one's husband or wife by a previous marriage'
Ex wife/husband
Surname, first name, middle name, Mr. Mrs. Ms. Miss
Family unit
Nuclear family: 'a social unit composed of father, mother, and children'.
Single child family, single mum, single dad
2.4 child family
DINK: 'double income no kids'
Extended family
Single mother/father, single parent family
Adopted, foster parents
Polygamy: 'the practice or condition of having more than one spouse, especially wife, at one time'.
Monogamy: 'marriage with only one person at a time'.
Family roles, house husband.

A: Hello to new students 5 minutes
Where is your hometown? What do you do here? Are you a student or do you have a job? Why are you learning English? Which country do you want to go to? Introduce yourself very briefly.

B: Brainstorm 10 minutes
All students will know the basics so get one person to tell you all the family members in one go *'Mother, father, sister, brother, aunt, uncle, grandmother and grandfather'*.
Once you have done that brainstorm on the topic. Aim to get more detailed vocabulary on the board.

C: Discussion

1: Think of and describe four <u>family units</u>. **15 minutes**
Make sure the students know what a family unit is and ask them to give you one example before you start.
Answer Check: Make a list on the board that they can use later and explain new concepts.

2: Ancestors (past tense) **10 minutes**
Talk about the oldest relative that you know about in your family.
Where did they live? What did they do? Do you know any interesting stories about them?

3: How many children would you like? Boy or girl? (*teacher's notes*) **10 minutes**
(T1: Age, T8: Romance, Marriage and Dating)

4: Should you <u>spoil</u> your child? (*teacher's notes*) **10 minutes**
How do you think spoiling your child will affect them in later life?
Answer Check

Breaktime (5 minutes)

5: How should you discipline your child? (*teacher's notes*) **10 minutes**
How were you disciplined as a child? What for? (past tense)

6: Single Parent Family: **10 minutes**
What effect does having one parent have on the child? Does it make a difference if it is a single mum or single dad?

7: DINK (double income no kids) **10 minutes**
These days this kind of relationship is becoming more common. What are the good and bad points of a DINK relationship and do you think you would prefer to have this kind of lifestyle? Why or why not?

D: Role Play:

Single parent job interview (*printables 1*) **10 minutes**
<u>Person A:</u> You are a single parent. You have a four year old child who you can now send to kindergarten although it is expensive. Go to a job interview for some simple office work. You haven't worked in a long time and really need this job. You have excellent skills and qualifications. You must get this job.

<u>Person B:</u> Employer.
You have many other people who are interested in this job. Ask interview questions but make the interview difficult for them.

What is their experience? Why do they want the job? When was the last time they worked? Will having a child affect their work? What if the child gets sick?

Household Chores (*printables 2*) **15 minutes**

First make a list on the board of the various chores that need to be done around the house. Make sure the roleplay is already written on the board or use the handout found in the printables.
Spend a five minutes explaining the activity and what each person in each role has to do.

'Interrupting': Make sure that the students know what this means.
Put them into threes. If you can't make one group then try a four with two parents and two children

Person A: Parent. You work late. Often you don't get any time to do the housework. You have two teenage children (B and C) who hardly do any chores to help around the house. They are extremely lazy.
B: Does some housework but not much. They put the dirty plates in the kitchen but never wash up. Sometimes they tidy their dirty clothes up.
C: Does nothing and is really untidy. They leave food and dirty clothes everywhere. They leave the lights on.

Be angry with them and tell them they must start to do the chores.

Person B: You do some housework but not much. Make it sound like you do more.
 Continually interrupt your brother/sister.

Person C: You never do anything. Take credit for what your brother/sister does. Say that you did it.
 Continually interrupt your brother/sister.

E: Drilling the vocabulary and finish

Family
Additional Questions and Activities

1: How are you similar to your parents? **10 minutes**
(T2: Personality)
Talk about their appearance and their character.

2: Adoption **10 minutes**
Does being adopted affect a person in later life?
If a person is adopted do you think they would be like their real parents or foster parents?

3: Do parents influence their children too much? **10 minutes**
Should teenagers be allowed to make their own decisions?

4: Would you consider staying single? Why or why not?   **5 minutes**
In China 'single' means you are not married.

5: Would you like to have an extended family? Why or why not?   **5 minutes**

6: What <u>makes</u> an excellent family?   **10 minutes**

7: What <u>makes</u> a good parent?   **10 minutes**
Would you make a good parent? Why or why not?

Devil's Advocate

The single child policy is an excellent way to manage the population.   **10 minutes**

You should not spoil your child.   **10 minutes**

Roleplay

Parent – Your Child (T1: Age)   **5 minutes**
<u>Person A:</u> Parent. You are not happy with your child.
They are watching too much TV, play too many computer games and never doing their homework (or if they are a teenager also you don't like their girlfriend/boyfriend).
<u>Person B:</u> Child. Disagree with your parent.

Going Abroad   **5 minutes**
You can put your students into pairs or groups of three for this.
<u>Person A:</u> Parent(s). You don't want your son/daughter to go abroad to study. You want them to stay and work in the family business. You hope they will marry a local Chinese person.
<u>Person B:</u> You have other plans. Disagree with your parents.

Retirement Home (*T1: Age, printables*)   **10 minutes**
<u>Person A:</u> You often work away from home. Your parents live in another city. You think your grandparents are too old to be left alone. Strongly encourage them to move to a nice old people's home.
Key words: *new friends, quiet, soft music, safe, nurses, soft food and new hobbies.*

<u>Person B:</u> Grandparent: You don't want to leave. You will feel lonely, miss your friends, routine and your family will forget about you. Refuse to leave. Be <u>stubborn</u>.

Cleaning Lady   **5 minutes**
<u>Person A:</u> You want to hire a cleaning lady every month to clean the apartment. Tell your family members.
<u>Person B:</u> Family member. No way! They should save money and do the cleaning themselves. Person A is always too lazy.

Family – Printables 1
Single Parent Job Interview

Person A: You are a single parent

You have a four year old child who you can now send to kindergarten although it is expensive.

Go to a job interview for some simple office work. You haven't worked in a long time and really need this job.

You have excellent skills and qualifications.

You must get this job.

Person B: Employer

You have many other people who are interested in this job.

Ask interview questions but make the interview difficult for them.

What is their experience? Why do they want the job? When was the last time they worked?

Will having a child affect their work?
What if the child gets sick?

Printables 2
Household Chores

Person A: Parent.

You work late. Often you don't get any time to do the housework.
You have two teenage children (**B and C**) who hardly do any chores to help around the house. They are extremely lazy.

B: Does some housework but not much. They put the dirty plates in the kitchen but never wash up. Sometimes they tidy their dirty clothes up.

C: Does nothing and is really untidy. They leave food and dirty clothes everywhere. They leave the lights on

Be angry with them and tell them they must start to do the chores.

Person B:

You do some housework but not much. Make it sound like you do more.

Continually interrupt your brother/sister and parent

Person C:

You never do anything. Take credit for what your brother/sister does. Say that you did it.

Continually interrupt your brother/sister and parent.

Family
Teacher's Notes

Out of all the topics this will be the most important for most of your students. In Asia and especially China, the whole culture revolves around the family.

The single child policy was introduced in 1978 in order to gain some control of the rapidly increasing population. Wealthy families can pay to have another child. This can be up to 40,000 RMB or 4,000 pounds/6,200 US dollars (2012).

Grandparents will often live with the family. They may take care of the kid(s) while the parents are off at work. They may look after them full time if the parents have to work in another city.

3: How many kids do you want?
Remind students that although they are Chinese, most will also be travelling to other countries. They may be able to find a partner and start a new life abroad therefore breaking free from the single child policy.

Girl or boy? Families will always hope to have a boy in a male dominated society as they will become the bread winner in the future.

It the past many families would 'throw their girl into the river' and try again for a boy. This sounds terrible but most cases of this would be in the countryside.
People living in rural areas form 70% of China's massive 1.3 billion population (though Chinese newspapers say its now 50%). It all seems barbaric but we must also remember that for many years conditions in the countryside were extremely bad with the only work being farming or labour. In the 'Great Leap Forward' 10 million people starved to death. A girl would have no hope of getting work and would have been seen as a huge extra burden on an already starving family. People would usually have no meat and if they had rice it would be saved for special times. These days, though it is still reported to be practiced in some places, generally families will keep their child whether boy or girl.

5: Should you spoil your child?
You will have mixed answers about this, but generally, in a country with the single child policy the students will say that "a girl may be spoilt and should learn to be dependent. She should be looked after and pampered as much as possible in order to become as desirable as possible to attract a good husband. The boy" however, "should learn to do things for themselves so that they can support the family in the future. The boy should not be spoilt".

6: How should you discipline your child?
It was common practice to beat your child in many parts of Asia including China, though this method of punishment has now ceased. Students have no problem talking about this in detail.

Topic 07 Friends

Part 2: Relationships

Friends

Vocabulary and useful stuff

Best friend, close friend
Old friend, life-long friend
Acquaintance
Colleague
Class mate
Room mate
Team mate
Net friend, pen pal
Mate, buddy
Friend of a friend
Lost touch with
Fallen out with

A: Hello to new students   5 minutes
Where is your hometown? What do you do here? Are you a student or do you have a job? Why are you learning English? Which country do you want to go to? Introduce yourself very briefly.

B: Brainstorm   10 minutes
Do a quick brainstorm to build up a list on the white board.
Make sure you talk about the difference between a friend and an acquaintance.

C: Discussion

1: What qualities should a best friend have?   10 minutes
Talk about your best friend. Include when and how you met and anything interesting you have done together. (past tense)

What things do you talk about or do with a best friend that you don't do with other friends?

2. How are friends different from family?   5 minutes
What things would you tell your friends and not your family? Why?

3. Tell a story that happened to you with your best friend when you were a child.
They maybe an old classmate or someone you used to play with.(past tense) **15 minutes**

4. Do you have any net friends? **10 minutes**
How many do you have? How did you meet them?
Are net friends real friends? How come?
Would you meet them in real life? Why or why not?

Breaktime (5 minutes)

5. Have you ever 'lost touch' with a friend? **10 minutes**
What happened? Where are they now? Could you find them?

6: Have you ever 'fallen out' with a friend? (past tense) **10 minutes**
What happened?
Did you manage to 'patch things up'? Are you friends now?

D: Devil's Advocate

Never go into business with a friend. **10 minutes**

E: Role Play:

Make a promise **10 minutes**
Part 1 (5 minutes)
Make sure the students know that this is a role play. Even though I'd written this on the board, one time a student told their classmate something that was real by accident. The look on their classmates face was a picture.

Person A: You have something important you want to tell your friend. Tell them what it is and make them promise you not to tell anyone. It is your secret.
Person B: Promise not to tell anyone.

Part 2 (5 minutes)
Person A: Your friend told someone. Now everyone knows. You are really angry with your friend. Ask them why they did it?
Person B: Make a good excuse and 'talk your way out of it'.

Borrow some money from an old friend (*printables 1*) **20 minutes**
(T15: Banks & Money)

Part 1: Small Talk (5 minutes)
Before you start tell the class that if you are Person A you must make 'small talk' before they ask for the money. Write it on the board and ask the class what they think it means:

talk about their family, you heard they had a baby, you heard that they got promoted, you heard that they bought a new car or talk about the weather.
Tell them that Person A must make small talk for at least two minutes before asking for the money.

Part 2: (10 minutes)
Person A: You really need some money. You asked the bank but they said no. However, you heard that recently an old friend won a lot of money on the lottery. Give them a call and ask if you can borrow some. Never give up. You need this money! Make small talk first.
Person B: You haven't heard from this person in five years; no e-mails; no calls or even any text messages. Why should you lend them any money?

Part 3: (5 minutes)
While they are doing part one, quickly write this up on the white board.
Person A: You kindly leant your friend the money but after six months you really need it back. Ask for it back.
Person B: Make excuses not to return it.

F: Drilling the vocabulary and finish

Friends - Additional Questions and Activities

1: They say "Everyone comes into your life for a reason".   **10 minutes**
Talk about a friend who has taught you something important, or helped you out in some way.

2: Describe someone you know who is popular.   **10 minutes**
Why do they have so many friends? What makes a person popular?

3: If your girlfriend/boyfriend's best friend was of the opposite sex, how would you feel? (T8 Romance, Marriage and Dating)   **5 minutes**
What would you do, especially if they were spending a lot of time together?

4. Is it important to have friends?   **5 minutes**

Roleplay

Only an acquaintance (*printables 2*)   **10 minutes**
(T17: Numbers & Quantities)

Person A: You are new in town. You don't have any friends and are lonely. However, yesterday you met someone in a coffee shop and got their telephone number. Phone up

and ask them to join you for lunch sometime. Be persistent. If they are busy think of another time.
Person B: You don't really know this person and <u>regret</u> giving them your telephone number. Make excuses not to meet them.

Room mates   **10 minutes**

An excellent way to finish a class. Its simple, fun and the students become quite animated. Do a quick-fire brainstorm asking individual students what terrible habits a room mate can have? Write a quick list on the board.
Borrow your toothbrush without asking, snore, talk in their sleep, bring their boyfriend/girlfriend back, leave food lying around, untidy, spend too long in the bathroom; the list is endless.

Person A: You dislike your new room mate and their terrible habits. Politely tell them they have to change.
Person B: Totally disagree with your room mate. You don't like them either.

Go into business with a friend   **10 minutes**
Person A: You want to turn your hobby into a business. Persuade your friend to join you.
Person B: You don't think it's a good idea. Think of reasons to say no.

Friends
Printables 1

Borrow some money from an old friend: Part 1

Person A:

You really need some money. You asked the bank but they said no. However, you heard that recently an old friend won a lot of money on the lottery. Give them a call and ask if you can borrow some. Never give up. You need this money!

You must make small talk before you ask for at least two minutes, for example,
talk about their family, you heard they had a baby, you heard that they got promoted, you heard that they bought a new car.

Person B:

You haven't heard from this person in five years; no e-mails; no calls or even any text messages.

Why should you lend them any money?

Printables 2
Only an acquaintance:

Person A:

You are new in town. You don't have any friends and are lonely. However, yesterday you met someone in a coffee shop and got their telephone number. <u>Phone up</u> and ask them to join you for lunch sometime. Be persistent. If they are busy think of another time.

Person B:

You don't really know this person and <u>regret</u> giving them your telephone number. Make excuses not to meet them.

Topic 08
Romance & Dating

Part 2: Relationships

Romance and Dating
Vocabulary and useful stuff

Spoken: my 'g/f' or 'b/f'
Long term relationship
An item, couple, my partner
Instant chemistry
Mr or Mrs Right
Compatible (as opposed to 'suitable')
Short term relationship
One night stand, a fling, seeing someone
An affair, lovers, adultery, mistress (there is no male equivalent)
Two-timing
Ex, split/ break up
Single, available, bachelor, left-over woman (a Chinese term for a single woman over 30)
'To sleep with' if a student isn't comfortable in using the word 'sex'
Celibate
Gay, lesbian and bisexual
Open relationship
Toy boy
A turn on, a turn off, fancy someone
A crush
Physical contact: hug, cuddle and embrace, holding hands, arm in arm, kiss
Hitting on someone, chatting someone up

A: Hello to new students   5 minutes
Where is your hometown? What do you do here? Are you a student or do you have a job? Why are you learning English? Which country do you want to go to? Introduce yourself very briefly.

B: Brainstorm   10 minutes
Ask each student in turn to brainstorm on the topic. This is normally quite fun. Whatever the student says, you can get their neighbour to explain what it means.
Try and build up some clear separate lists on the white board for the students to use.

Introduce the word 'partner' as something you will use throughout the lesson.

Ask them what age does a boy become a man and a girl become a woman? (T1: Age)
Let them discuss it for two minutes.
Answer Check: Students may often refer to a man in their mid to late 20's as a 'boy'. Ask the female students if they want to date a man/guy or a boy?

C: Discussion

1: In China, girlfriend and boyfriend is the usual type of relationship.   **10 minutes**
Think of five more forms of relationship. There may already be something from the brainstorm up on the white board that you can use as an example.
Answer Check: Build a list up on the white board after the discussion.

2: How can you <u>tell</u> if someone is interested in you?   **10 minutes**
Eye contact, they make conversation, ask for your number, send you messages, ask about you to your friends etc

or **How can you get someone interested in you?**
Find out their interests, be in the same place as them, make them laugh etc

3: Think of five things you should or shouldn't do on a first date?   **10 minutes**
Answer Check

4: What things do you find attractive in the opposite sex?   **10 minutes**
Explain the term 'turn on' and 'turn off'.
They can talk about personality and physical appearance.

Breaktime (5 minutes)

5: Would you go on a blind date? Why or why not?   **10 minutes**
Why do people go on blind dates?

6: BTQ: What is the most important to you in a partner?   **10 minutes**
Money, Appearance or Love? Why?
Students have to rate each one using percentages, for example, *Love 60%, Appearance 20% and Money 20%*.
Some may change the question if they want, for example, by adding personality. This is ok. It is their discussion to do with it what they want.
Answer check.

7: Would you live with your partner before getting married?   **10 minutes**
Why or why not?
What are the advantages and disadvantages of living with your partner only after marriage?

8: What are the three most romantic things you could give or do for your partner?
    10 minutes
If you have a small class you can do an answer check and write one idea from each student on the white board. You can then give them two minutes to discuss the most romantic one and why? Each student votes for their favourite.

D: Devil's Advocate

It's ok for couples to kiss and cuddle in public places.   **10 minutes**

E: Role Play:

Foreign partner   **10 minutes**
Person A: You are a student studying abroad. You have a foreign partner now and have been living together for six months. Phone your parents and tell them.
Person B: Parents: No way! You don't want a foreign person in your family. You are very traditional.

F: Drilling the vocabulary and finish

Romance & Dating
Additional Questions and Activities

1: Do you believe in love at first sight? Why or why not?   **5 minutes**

2: What are the symptoms of love?   **5 minutes**
Use symptoms of a cold as an example.

3: Describe the qualities in your perfect partner.   **10 minutes**
　　Is it possible to find Mr or Mrs Right? Why or why not?

4: Who should pay the bill on a date? (T15: Banks and Money)   **10 minutes**
Should men pay for everything? What should the woman pay for?

5: BTQ: Online Dating   **10 minutes**
These days looking for a partner online has become very popular.
Why do people look for a partner online?
Would you look for your loved one on the internet? Why or why not?
Is it possible to find a genuine partner on the internet? Why or why not?

6: Have you ever had a crush on someone before? (past tense)   **5 minutes**
Maybe someone you liked but never told them. How did they make you feel?

7: Would you consider having a foreign partner? Why or why not?   **10 minutes**
Already used in the role play, but becomes more thorough in terms of a discussion.
What are the positives and negative sides to having a foreign partner?

8: Romantic Candlelit Dinner (T19: Cooking)   **10 minutes**
If you were going to cook a romantic dinner for your partner what would it be? Why would you choose it? What would dessert be?
or
If you were going to take your partner to a restaurant for a romantic candlelit dinner, where would it be? Why would you choose to go there?

9: Quick fire from the teacher asking individual students   **5 minutes**
Would you like it if your boyfriend was shorter than you? Why or why not?
Would you mind if your girlfriend was taller than you? Why or why not?
Would you like it if your girlfriend had an athletic build?
Would you like it of your girlfriend was older than you? (toy boy)
                  boyfriend was younger than you? Why or why not?

10: If your girlfriend/boyfriend's best friend was of the opposite sex, how would you feel? (T7: Friends)   **5 minutes**

11: Should you always be honest to your partner?   **5 minutes**
Are there any things you would not tell your partner?
Are there any things you would tell your friends but not your partner?

Devil's Advocate

China should have a more modern approach to dating and relationships. 10 minutes
Remind the students to use the examples on the white board, including living together before marriage.

Men should pay for everything on a date!   **10 minutes**
You really need a class with equal number of male and female students for this.
It's also possible to put one male student against two girls or visa versa if their English is pretty good or they are very outspoken and love arguing. It's a matter of getting to know your students.

Money is the most important thing to consider in any relationship.   **10 minutes**

It doesn't matter about appearance. It's the personality that is important in a partner.   **10 minutes**

Students should not be allowed to have girlfriends or boyfriends in middle school or high school.
(It's often dissuaded in China.)   **10 minutes**

Roleplay

Can't find a partner   **10 minutes**

Person A: You have no luck finding a girlfriend or boyfriend. Ask your friend for advice.
Person B: You have lots of experience. Give your friend some tips. Maybe it's their appearance, personality or the way they are going about it.

I have a big crush   **10 minutes**

Person A: You have a huge crush on someone. You see them every day. They drive you crazy. You can't eat and you can't sleep.
They are very popular and you don't know how you can get their interest.
Ask your friend for advice.
Person B: You have lots of experience. Give your friend some tips on how to be successful.

Parents not happy (T1: Age)   **5 minutes**

In pairs or threes
Person A& B: Parents are not happy with son/daughters boyfriend/girlfriend.
Person C: Son/Daughter: You love your bf/gf and you don't want to leave them. Argue with your parents.

Romance & Dating
Teacher's Notes

Before you start teaching this lesson, being armed with some basic info on Chinese attitudes to dating is more than useful.

Your students
Firstly, if you are teaching college students there is a high chance that many of them won't have had sex before even if they are in a relationship. Some may say they have never had a girlfriend or boyfriend. Parents strongly influence their children not to get involved in relationships until school has finished. At college, it is also discouraged as they think it detracts from focusing on study and hard work. If a student has a girlfriend or boyfriend then they may not tell the parents about it until much later.

In terms of any other form of relationship other than girlfriend and boyfriend working towards marriage, it will certainly be a minority in China. Extra marital relationships, like many other countries are common place though.

Parents
Parents influence their children strongly and if they disapprove of a girlfriend or boyfriend they will say no to it. Normally what they say goes and its end of argument.

Parents' approval will largely depend on income, savings and back ground of their son or daughters partner. It is common for parents to strongly pressure their son or daughter to divorce if their spouse isn't earning enough money.

Approach to dating
Your students will always be very interested in the differences between dating in their country and yours. Adding five minutes of teacher talk time to explain how 'we' do it in the West is never wasted time.

In China if you 'like' someone you should start sending multiple text messages as often as possible to show your interest; 'like' being the Asian equivalent of 'to fancy' someone. The guy should give his date small gifts or even flowers and definitely pay for everything. If they agree they like each other then they will hangout as much as possible though it may be a no sex relationship.

They will normally try and stay together and aim for marriage. Some people still wait until after marriage until they live and sleep together. A Chinese person will normally only ever had one or two partners at the most.

Generally speaking, casual sex is not common in China.

Topic 09: Marriage & Divorce

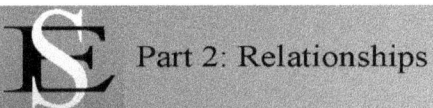 Part 2: Relationships 09

Marriage & Divorce

Vocabulary and useful stuff

Down on one knee, propose
Stag night, hen night
Best man
Bridesmaids
Arranged marriage
Spouse
Split up, break up
Separate, divorce, live apart
Adultery, unfaithful
An affair, lovers, mistress (there is no male equivalent)

A: Hello to new students   5 minutes
Where is your hometown? What do you do here? Are you a student or do you have a job? Why are you learning English? Which country do you want to go to? Introduce yourself very briefly.

B: Brainstorm   10 minutes
A quick brainstorm to build up a list on the white board.

C: Discussion

1: Describe your ideal husband or wife?   10 minutes
Talk about personality and also if they should adopt traditional roles at home *for example* the wife should do all the cooking and shopping. The husband should be the bread winner.

2: BTQ: Describe the last wedding you went to (past tense)   10 minutes
Who's wedding? When and where was it? Did you enjoy it? Were there many people there? What did the bride wear? Describe the party.

3: When is the best age to get married? Why? (T1: Age)   10 minutes
Answer Check

4: Girls: What kind of wedding ring do you want? Describe it?   5 minutes
    Material, plain, diamond, gold, platinum, how expensive?
  Men: What kind of wedding ring would you buy your wife? How much would you pay for it?
Should you both have a wedding ring or just the wife?

5: What kind of wedding party would you like? (future tense)   **10 minutes**
(T10: Parties)
Would you like it to be in a restaurant or hotel? Maybe something different? Describe music, decoration, food and the speech.

Breaktime (5 minutes)

6: Where would you like to go on your honeymoon? Why?   **10 minutes**
It could be in another country. Which city? What activities would you do there?

7: Parental Influence   **10 minutes**
Should parents be able to influence who their son or daughter should marries?
Many people leave their partner because their parents say so. Would you do what your parents told you to? What if you really loved your partner or were already married to them?

8: Why do people get divorced?   **15 minutes**
Surely they love each other and are positive that their partner 'is the one'.
After all, marriage is for life.
Answer Check

D: Devil's Advocate

Marriage is the end of love   **10 minutes**

E: Role Play: 10 minutes

Person A: Parent. You think you have found a suitable partner for your son/daughter to start dating with an aim to get marriage. Strongly encourage this relationship.
Person B: Son/daughter. Strongly disagree with your parents. You don't like this person and you have other ideas.

F: Drilling the vocabulary and finish

Marriage & Divorce
Additional Questions and Activities

1: Why is getting married important?   **10 minutes**
In the West, many people live together but don't get married. Some even have children.

2: How do you keep the love alive after a long time in a marriage?   **5 minutes**

3: Would you marry someone who had been divorced? If not, why not?   **10 minutes**
What if they had been divorced twice?

4: Would you consider staying single? Why or why not?   **5 minutes**
What are the advantages and disadvantages of staying single?

5: Think of three signs that a marriage is not working?   **10 minutes**

6: Why is the divorce rate so high these days?   **10 minutes**

7: Would you 'stand by' your partner no matter even if they make mistakes?
How far would you support your husband or wife? What if they lost their job or were not successful?   **10 minutes**

8: How does a relationship change when a couple gets married?   **10 minutes**
This means from girlfriend and boyfriend to husband and wife.

Devil's Advocate

There should be a tough law for people who commit adultery   **10 minutes**

Roleplay

Plan a stag or hen night for your friend   **10 minutes**
<u>Person A:</u> You are getting married soon. Ask your best friend to plan a great evening for you. It must be interesting and great fun; a night to remember for the rest of your life.
<u>Person B:</u> Think about location, music, food and drink and something special that will happen during the evening.

Marriage guidance councilor   **15 minutes**
This really deserves to be in the main lesson plan. However, this does need the class to be in groups of three with at least two people in each group being the same sex.
You can always have people working in twos though they may feel somewhat left out when the rest of the class start arguing with each other.
If you decide to do this roleplay, start to mentally prepare yourself for who will be in each group during break time.

Part 1 (5 minutes)
Explain what a marriage guidance councilor is.
What problems can a marriage have? Brainstorm with the class and make a list on the white board. Have the second part below, already written on the board in advance so you can start the roleplay immediately.

Part 2 (10 minutes)
Person A: Marriage guidance councilor. You are an expert at helping couples with their problems. Give them some advice on saving their marriage.
Persons B and C: You have been together for only one year and already you have difficulties. Blame each other for your problems.

Parents don't like your partner **5 minutes**

Person A: Parent. You never liked your son/daughter's partner. They have been married for one year and they aren't making enough money. They have a low position at work. You have decided that they should divorce. Tell your son or daughter.
Person B: Your partner is a really nice person. Disagree with your parents.

Marriage & Divorce - Teacher's Notes

Things are done very differently in China to in the western world. A couple will first be legally married in an office. Where this takes place depends their 'hukou' which is the legal province of birth, for example, if neither are from Beijing, it means they cannot register in Beijing and will have to leave town to sign on the dotted line. This is a formal occasion with no ceremony or witnesses.

After this, the couple will have a wedding party to cement their marriage. Normally this will be in a restaurant in a hotel. Friends, family and colleagues will be invited. It is obligatory for colleagues and friends to bring cash in a red envelope to hand to the couple.

Red has always been the traditional Chinese colour for the bride to wear though these days many are choosing the white dress instead.

Divorce
It's easier and more common to get divorced in China these days. Normally divorce will have something to do with money or the couple's ability to have children.
If either are not making enough money to support their child after it's born, the parents may pressure the couple to get a divorce.

It is seen as unfavourable to marry someone who is divorced in China. If they have been married twice this is a definite 'no no'.

Topic 10 Parties

Part 2: Relationships

Parties

Vocabulary and useful stuff

Host
Halloween, fancy dress party
House party, illegal party, warehouse party
House warming, house leaving party
Stag and hen night
25th silver, 50th golden, 75th diamond wedding anniversary
Party animal, party pooper
Gate-crasher, bouncer, doorman
Club, clubbing, going out on the town
Pub, bar
Stamina, staying power, lightweight

Teachers Party Tips: (*printables*) Gradually make a list of these six points throughout the lesson. You can also give them the printable version at the end of the lesson to take home.

A: Hello to new students   5 minutes
Where is your hometown? What do you do here? Are you a student or do you have a job? Why are you learning English? Which country do you want to go to? Introduce yourself very briefly.

B: Brainstorm (*teacher's notes*)   10 minutes
After a couple of minutes ask the students to think of five other types of party. When you answer check get them to describe each one and make a list on the white board.

C: Discussion

1: BTQ: Describe the best party you ever went to. (past tense)   **10 minutes**
When, where, what was the party for? What made it special?
You could also talk about the last party you went to. Was it a good or bad one? Why?

2: What kind of person are you?   **10 minutes**
Are you sociable and love parties or do you prefer to have a quiet time? How come?

3: Open discussion on drinking   **15 minutes**
Ask one student to tell you ten types of soft drink and count them down. Tell their classmates not to help unless they really can't think of anything.
Ask someone in the class to think of five alcoholic drinks and write them on the board.

You only need to make a small list: *White and red wine, spirits, cocktails, punch.*
The list can be endless so keep thinks minimal. Make a list on the board and explain some of them, for example, a cocktail is spirit and a soft drink combined.

4: Have you ever drunk alcohol before? If not, why not? (past tense)   **10 minutes**
If you did, did you enjoy it? Where, when, who with and what happened?
Have you been drunk before? Tell your story.

Breaktime (5 minutes)

5: What kind of wedding party would you like? (future tense)   **10 minutes**
(T9: Marriage and Divorce)
Would it be in a restaurant or hotel? Maybe something different? Describe music, decoration, food and the speech.

6: Do you like going to clubs? Why or why not?   **10 minutes**
What is the difference between a club and a bar?
Describe the last time you went to a club (or bar for anyone that hasn't been to a club before). Did you enjoy it? Describe your night out.

D: Role Play:

Plan an <u>evening out</u> for your boss   **10 minutes**
<u>Person A:</u> Employee. Your boss has asked you to plan a special evening out for him and some important foreign clients. Tell him your ideas. <u>Impress</u> your boss.
<u>Person B:</u> Boss. You want to impress your clients. Continually make changes to this plan.

Persuade your friend   **10 minutes**
(T2: Personality)
<u>Person A:</u> You are a student on a Western campus. You have been invited out to a party. You don't want to go alone. Persuade your friend to go with you.
<u>Person B:</u> Friend. You are very shy. Make excuses not to go, for example, *too busy, don't like smoking, drinking, too noisy, dangerous, too late and don't like clubs*

Gate-crasher   **15 minutes**
Explain what a 'gate-crasher', 'doorman' and 'bouncer' is.
If you can, put your students into small groups.
<u>Person A and B:</u> Gatecrashers. You have no ticket or invitation to get into the party. Try and persuade the doorman to let you in. Be persistent.
<u>Person C:</u> Doorman. Refuse to let anyone in with no initiation or ticket. You are not allowed to accept money.

E: Drilling the vocabulary and finish

Parties
Additional Questions and Activities

Roleplay

Plan a <u>stag</u> or <u>hen night</u> for your friend　　　　　　　　　　**10 minutes**
<u>Person A:</u> You are getting married soon. Ask your best friend to plan a great evening for you. It must be interesting and great fun; a night to remember for the rest of your life.
<u>Person B:</u> Think about location, music, food and drink and something special that will happen during the evening.

Drunk Driving　　　　　　　　　　**5 minutes**
(T16: Giving Directions)
<u>Person A:</u> Police officer. You have caught this person drunk driving. You hate people who do this. Take them down to the police station immediately.
<u>Person B:</u> Drunk driver. Make some big excuses and try and avoid punishment

Noisy Neighbours　　　　　　　　　　**5 minutes**
<u>Person A:</u> Your neighbours are having a very loud party next door and its 2.00am. Ask them to turn down the music. You have an important day at work tomorrow.
<u>Person B:</u> Neighbour. Make excuses not to turn it down. It will spoil your party.

Parents　　　　　　　　　　**5 minutes**
<u>Person A and B:</u> Parents. You don't want your teenage son/daughter going to that terrible college party. Say no!
<u>Person C:</u> Son/daughter. You really want to go. Everyone will be going. You must go!

Parties - Printables

Teacher's handy party tips

These are designed as <u>life savers</u> for anyone who has not been on a typical Western party. Follow these tips for an enjoyable night or ignore them at your peril.

A good night out may start at around 9.00pm at a pub or bar and then on to a club at around midnight. At 2.00am people may go to a house party until 5.00am

1: Always make sure you eat well before you go out. Chinese girls often have a habit of eating hardly anything such as an apple, biscuits or yogurt as their evening meal.

2: Go late. Arrive at 10pm. This has two benefits. Firstly, when you get there, everyone else will be drunk with a long night ahead of them. You will leave the pub/bar feeling really nice after a few drinks and ready to dance. Secondly, when you arrive you will be the most popular person who everyone will want to talk to. Other people in the bar may notice this too.

3: Never mix your drinks. If you are used to it, then this is fine. If you are not used to drinking much, stay with the same drink. If you mix your drinks you may be quickly sick and wanting to go home. Remember the night will be a long one.

4: When you are at the party, if there is punch don't drink it. If someone offers it politely say no. You don't know what is in it. Punch can be dangerous.

5: Never fall asleep at a party. If you are falling asleep and you can't stop yourself go home. For a woman it can be dangerous. For anyone, you can become a target for people's amusement.

Parties
Teacher's Notes

Students: Your students' notion of what a party is will be completely different from yours. When you brainstorm different types of party most students' answers will be limited to say the least. This is definitely a time where the teacher can educate the students in other ways other than helping them practice their English, especially for those that will be going abroad and spending life on campus. Lord help them! Your students will be totally unaware of the riotous nature of a typical Western house party. Whether it's a student party or for older people, the results will often be the same; a two day hang over followed by flashbacks of things you wish you never did. Chinese folk never experience this extreme form of behaviour so it is definitely your job to prepare them.

Make sure they take notes and try and paint a clear picture of what Western people do when they go out and party. Try and mix advice with discussion equally using the 'Teacher's Handy Party Tips' in the printables section; perhaps a few minutes of teacher talk time after each discussion. You can give this print off to your students as they leave rather than at the beginning of class, otherwise they will spend ten minutes reading it with their heads down.

Drinking
Be aware this strongly overlaps with Topic 1 Drink and Drugs, Kick-Ass Lesson Plans - TEFL Discussion Questions and Activities China Part 2, but what is a party without drinking right? This can also be found in the teacher's notes of that topic.

Most of your class won't have done much drinking in their lives. Students will have hardly drunk anything let alone getting drunk. Some will say they have never drunk anything, even a beer. As a result, it's best making discussion points as flexible and therefore as answerable as possible:

Have you ever drunk alcohol before? If not why not?
If you did, did you enjoy it? Where, when, who with and what happened?
Have you been drunk before? Tell your story.

If you say "Have you ever had a drink before?" this may confuse some students so you need to explain that 'a drink' means to drink alcohol. It is the students' habit to use the word 'alcohol' as often as possible in this topic. Also, because most will have had little or no drinking experience, if possible put them into groups of three otherwise the discussion may finish after two minutes. Get them to focus on practicing their past tense as many will not be interested in this topic.

Drinking Vocabulary: Red and white wine (often confused with Chinese 'Baijiu' which also translates to 'white wine'. Students may refer to them as 'grape wine'.
Spirits, soft drinks, punch, cocktails, a pint, a slammer, a depth charge.

Topic 11 Houses & Apartments

Part 3: House & Home

Houses & Apartments

Vocabulary and useful stuff

A property
Apartment (US), flat (UK)
Mortgage
To let, rent, deposit, three months rent in advance, contract
Landlord/lady, estate agent
Tenant
Furnished, semi furnished, unfurnished
City centre, suburbs, countryside

Detached, semi detached, terraced house, a terrace
Hallway, landing
Living room, lounge (British)
W.C. the john, wash room, rest room (US), the loo, bathroom (British)
Conservatory
Loft, attic

Ground floor, first floor, second floor (UK)
First floor, second floor (US) The floor at ground level is the first floor
The downstairs, the upstairs
Basement

A: Hello to new students   5 minutes
Where is your hometown? What do you do here? Are you a student or do you have a job? Why are you learning English? Which country do you want to go to? Introduce yourself very briefly.

B: Brainstorm   10 minutes
A quick five minute brainstorm on the topic to start off the class.
You can also go from student to student asking them to think of one place we can live in, for example, hotel, villa, cottage or hospital if you are very ill. Make a list on the board. .

C: Discussion

1: What are the advantages and disadvantages of renting or buying an apartment?
15 minutes

Go through any important vocabulary beforehand such as *mortgage, to let, rent, deposit, three weeks rent in advance, contract, landlord/lady, estate agent and tenant.*

Make it clear to the class that this is actually four questions in one and they should answer thoroughly.

2: BTQ: **Describe where you grew up as a child** (past tense)   **10 minutes**
Before you start, go through the meaning of 'city centre, suburbs' and 'countryside' then elicit using a small diagram on the board. This can be three circles, one inside the other, with the centre being the city centre, the middle band being suburbia and the outer being the countryside.
Students could also talk about the rooms in their house, their bedroom, the view out of their window and the games they played in their childhood.

3: City centre, suburbs or countryside?   5 minutes
Which area would you most like to live in and why?

4: Location   10 minutes
Think of five things that are important when choosing the location of a new property.
Answer Check: You should make a list of this on the white board as it will be useful in the role play later.
Answers can be positive or negative, for example, convenient/inconvenient to catch the subway, bus, noisy, quiet, dangerous or safe etc.

Breaktime (5 minutes)

5: Open questions to the class eliciting more vocabulary about rooms in the house.
    10 minutes
It may help to a quick drawing of a house on the whiteboard to help elicit.
Ask one student to tell you all the rooms downstairs and another to tell you all the rooms upstairs. They should know most of these. Vocabulary they may not know could be: *Detached, semi detached, terraced house, a terrace, hallway, landing, lounge (British English for living room), the john/restroom/washroom (US), bathroom/the loo (common British English for toilet), conservatory, loft, and attic.*

6: Describe your dream house   10 minutes
Where, which town, which country, what would the view be like from the window, how many rooms. Describe the rooms and what would be in each one?

7: Write down six adjectives to describe a property (*printables 1*)   10 minutes
Give examples before they get going; *spacious, cramped, bright, dark.*
Remind them that there are positive and negatives.
Answer Check: When they have finished write a list on the board. If you don't have enough board space, get them to write them down as you do an answer check.

8: Sharing accommodation   **10 minutes**
Have you or do you share your accommodation?
Do you like it?
What are the good and bad points of sharing?

This can be used with roleplay you could add to the end of the class if you have enough time so write a few of the bad points on the board if you have the space, for example, *they snore, they go to bed too late, they borrow things without asking.*
The role play can be found in the additional questions and activities.

D: Role Play:

Renting Accommodation (*printables 2*)   **20 minutes**

Part 1:   (10 minutes)
Encourage students to use the location list and the list of adjectives you have kept on the whiteboard.

Person A: You will start your new job soon and have just arrived in town. You don't have much money. 'Phone up' and agent and ask them to help you find suitable accommodation. It can't be too expensive.
Person B: Estate Agent. Try and let your worst accommodation to them. Make it sound much better than it is, for example, *if it's a basement say it is cool in the summer or private. If it's in a noisy area then say it is in a busy or active area.*

Part 2:   (10 minutes)
While the students are doing Part 1 write this up on the white board.
Keep the roles the same.

Person A: After one month, you have many problems with the apartment, for example, broken windows, broken furniture. Ask the agent to come and fix the problems.
Person B: Agent. You want to save money. Make excuses not to fix the problems.

E: Drilling the vocabulary and finish

Houses & Apartments
Additional Questions and Activities

1: Describe accommodation of the future (future tense)   **10 minutes**
Talk about how each room would be different. Set a time frame, say in fifty years time.

2: How many different places have you lived? (past tense)   **10 minutes**
This really means homes, but could be extended to other things like hotels. Be specific at the beginning of the discussion though.
If someone has only lived in one place, get them to listen to their partner and ask them questions, for example, When did you live there, where was it, which part of the country, was it an apartment, how old were you when you lived there, which one did you prefer, when did you move and why?

3: Describe the good and bad things about where you live.   **10 minutes**
Similar to Question 4 in the main lesson plan 'important things when choosing a location'.

4: Do you prefer older buildings to modern ones? Why?   **5 minutes**

5: Describe a building that you really like or think is <u>impressive</u>.   **10 minutes**
Why do you like it?
It could be in the students' hometown, present location or somewhere famous around the world. Students could also talk about a building they dislike.

6: City centre, suburbs or countryside?   **10 minutes**
What are the advantages and disadvantages of living in each one?
Answer Check

7: House Prices   **15 minutes**
People say that house prices are too high these days. Why are apartments so expensive? What effect does high house prices have on families? What can be done to solve this problem?

Roleplay

Room mates   **10 minutes**
An excellent way to finish a class. It's simple, fun and the students become quite animated. Students should already have done the prep' for this with Q8: Sharing accommodation and there should be a few examples of the bad habits a room mate may have on the white board.
Borrow your toothbrush without asking, snore, talk in their sleep, bring their boyfriend/girlfriend back, leave food lying around, untidy, spend too long in the bathroom; the list is endless.

<u>Person A:</u> You dislike your new room mate and their terrible habits. Politely tell them they have to change.

Person B: Totally disagree with your room mate. You don't like them either.

Noisy Neighbours (*printables 3*)   **10 minutes**

Person A: Your neighbours keep you awake all the time. At 6.30am they have loud children's TV on and until 2.30am they have loud action movies on. You get no sleep and your boss has noticed at work. Complain to the neighbours. Make them turn it down. Be very polite.
Person B: Neighbour. Refuse to turn down your TV.

Parking Space   **10 minutes**

You will need to explain to your students that in Western countries, people often have their own parking space outside their house. They may not own this space, but it is accepted that this is their area and no one else should park there.

Person A: Your neighbours continually park in your parking space outside your house. It's really inconvenient and annoying. Go to their house and ask them to move their car.
Person B: Neighbour. You have two cars. You have to park it there. Make excuses not to move it.

Cleaning Lady   **10 minutes**

Part 1   (5 minutes)
Person A: You want to hire a cleaning lady every month to clean the apartment. Tell your family members.
Person B: Family member. No way! They should save money and do the cleaning themselves. Person A is always too lazy.

Part 2   (5 minutes)
Person A: You hired a cleaner for the apartment but they did a really bad job. Tell them what they did wrong and that they should do it again.
Person B: Cleaner. Disagree. You think you did a good job. You just want to get paid and go home.

Houses & Apartments
Printables 1

Adjectives describing property:

Spacious, large, wide
Small, cramped, narrow
Cozy, snug, comfortable, quaint

Light, bright
Dark, dingy, gloomy

Damp, dank, musty, gloomy depressing

Clean
Untidy, shabby

Modern, new, luxury,
contemporary
Old, outdated

Beautiful, stunning, fabulous, charming
Ugly, unsightly, nasty

Printables 2

Renting Accommodation:

Person A:

You will start your new job soon and have just arrived in town. You don't have much money.

Phone up an agent and ask them to help you find suitable accommodation.

It can't be too expensive.

Person B: Estate Agent.

Try and let-out your **worst** accommodation to them.

Make it sound much better than it is, for example,
       if it is a basement say it is cool in the summer or private
       if it is in a noisy area say it is in a busy/active area.

Printables 3

Noisy Neighbours:

Person A: You can't get to sleep.

Your neighbours always have their TV turned on too loud.

Your boss noticed you look tired. You cannot concentrate on your work.

At 6.00am they have children's TV on very loud.
At 2.30am they have loud action films on very loud.

You have already asked them to turn it down.

Go and ask them to turn it down again.

Never give up.

Person B: Neighbours.

Think of reasons not to turn down your TV.

Topic 12: Describing Objects

Has half an hour of essential basic vocabulary building that is used through the lesson.
The teacher needs to prepare some objects in advance and bring them into class.

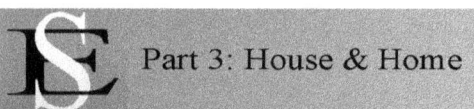

Part 3: House & Home

Describing Objects

A: Hello to new students   5 minutes
Where is your hometown? What do you do here? Are you a student or do you have a job? Why are you learning English? Which country do you want to go to? Introduce yourself very briefly.

B: Vocabulary and useful stuff (*printables*)   30 minutes
You need to build up a useful list of vocab' on the board that the students can use throughout the lesson.
The most important thing here is to keep the students attention and not allowing them to drift off. <u>Eliciting as much as possible will do the trick.</u>

Ask the students what are the most important things we need to consider when describing and object? Hold up any object available such as a pen or phone as a visual aid.
There are at least six
1: Shape
2: Colour
3: Size
4: Texture
5: Material
6: Function
As soon as a student says one of the above, go through it on the white board. Once you have finished, ask them what the next one is until you have all six up on the board.

You can give them the printed sheet to look at, but if you have room on your white board it's much better. They really need everything on the board to look at later.

1: Shape. Flat, 2-dimensional (*printables*)
Draw the shapes on the left of the board. Go through each noun and then get them to tell you the adjectives after.
Circle, circular
Triangle, triangular
Rectangle, rectangular
Square, squared
Ellipse, elliptical

Ask one of the students:
What is a square?
What is a circle?

Volumes: 3-dimensional (*printables*)
Go through each noun and then the adjectives
Sphere, spherical
Cylinder, cylindrical
Pyramid, pyramidal
Cone, conical
Oval, ovoid
Cube, cubic, a 3-D rectangle is called a cuboid

2: Colour
All students know their basic red, blue, yellow etc….including light and dark colours
Give them a few new types of color. I bring some examples of each; magazines are excellent for this.
Turquoise, lemon yellow, yellow ochre, crimson, burgundy, lime-green are easy colours to demonstrate.

3: Size
Forget measurements like cm's; this is spoken English. Instead we use comparisons to other things; we can say 'it's as big as a mobile phone'. Ask students to give examples.

4: Texture
How an object feels. We actually don't use too many words in spoken English to describe texture so don't get bogged down with this. *Hard, soft, rough smooth* are the ones we use mostly. *Sticky and spongy* are also useful.

5: Material
Again this is really simple. In terms of spoken English we use *glass, wood, paper, metal, cloth, plastic and stone*. This can also be divided up into *man-made and natural materials*.

6: Function
What an object does. It may have more than one function like a mobile phone.

C: Discussion & Activities

1: Guessing Game 1   15 minutes
In pairs, though three people is still ok.
Person A: Think of one object you would find at home. Don't tell your partner.
Person B: Ask your friend questions about it. Think about the vocabulary on the board, for example, How big is it? What material is it?
Person A: Answer each question simply. **You are not allowed to talk about function.** This includes which room the object is in. If you talk about function in any way, then it is too easy to guess the object.

Breaktime (10 minutes)
Breaktime is early. You need enough time for the next activity.

2: Guessing Game 2 (*teacher's notes*) **20 minutes**
You should bring a bag and at least ten items for this. Keep it to twenty minutes even if some students haven't had a go. This one of the few activities where students have to stand up in front of the class. As a teacher you should support them if they get stuck.

Student: Pick a student. Take them outside the classroom. They should put their hand in the bag and choose an object. They can't look inside the bag otherwise they will see all the other objects. They should look at the object and remember its qualities then return to the classroom. Teacher replaces the object into the bag so the class can't see it. You can show it later when they have guessed what it is.
The student should stand up in front of the class and describe their object using all the vocabulary on the board. **They should not mention function, including where it would be found, for example, in the kitchen.**

Class: The class should listen to what the student says and try and guess what the object is. They can ask questions and ask the student to repeat what they have just said.
The person to guess the object takes a turn to pick another object from the bag.
Repeat the exercise as many times as you can according within the allocated time.

3: BTQ: Describe an object of <u>sentimental value</u>. (past tense) **10 minutes**
Give an example of something you have that is important to you.
Tell the students to stop using the white board vocabulary. Tell them to think of an object they have that is important to them but may not necessarily be expensive.
Why is it important? Who gave it to them? When? Tell its story.

4: BTQ: Describe the last gift you gave someone. (past tense) **10 minutes**
(T13: Shopping)
Who for? What occasion was it? Why did you choose it? Where did you buy it from?

Describe the last gift you received from someone. Who gave it to you and when? Did you like it? Why did they give it to you?

D: Role Play:

Sell your multi functional product (*printables 2*) **20 minutes**
Students work in small groups of 3 or 4
Print off and prepare the flash cards found in Printables 2. Each one has a product on it.
Each student to take one of the product cards from the bag.
They have no time to prepare other than maybe find a word in their dictionaries.

Person A: Your company has made a new product. It has more than one function. Describe what it does to the bosses of a big supermarket and sell them your idea.
Person B and C: Ask questions. Why is this product better than other ones? Why should you buy this product?

Make sure each student gets to try and sell their product.

Give them an example. I always use a white board marker:
"This pen is amazing! It has more than one function. It has twenty colours and will only run out after one year. It is environmentally friendly as you can refill it again. It has a light on it so you can write in the dark and a radio in it so you can play music. It has an Mp3 so you can use it on the bus or train to listen to your favourite sounds. It has a small heater in it so it will keep your hand warm in the winter. Buy two; one for each hand. Amazing!"

E: Drilling the vocabulary and finish

Describing Objects
Additional Questions and Activities

Rooms and their contents: This links with Topic 11 Houses and Apartments.

1: What rooms does a house have upstairs and downstairs? **10 minutes**
Students should know this but may not know *hallway, landing, lounge (British English for living room), the john, the loo (common British English for toilet), conservatory, loft, and attic*. Draw a simple picture of a house on the white board to help illustrate this.

2: Ask individual students to tell you five things you may find in each room
For example, *lounge: TV, sofa, coffee table, DVD player, book shelf.* **5 minutes**

3: Think of at least six key words for any <u>household appliance</u> **5 minutes**
For example, *washing machine or microwave oven.* Students should write their words down and make a list. They may use their dictionaries to help them.

Role Play:

Buying a household appliance **20 minutes**

Part 1: (10 minutes)
Students to write six key words for using a washing machine, for example, *washing powder, turn on and off, hot and cold water, temperature, wash and dry.*
<u>Person A:</u> You want to buy a new washing machine. Ask the shop assistant how you use it and other important things you may need to know.
<u>Person B:</u> Shop assistant. Tell the customer about this appliance. Some safety tips would also be useful. Use the key words to help you.

Part 2: (10 minutes)
<u>Person A:</u> You can't get your washing machine to work and you damaged some of your clothes. Ask the shop assistant what went wrong?
<u>Person B:</u> Shop assistant. It is definitely not the washing machine that has a problem. Tell the customers what they did wrong.

Describing Objects
Printables 1

2 Dimensional or flat shapes:
Write the noun and adjective under each shape

Noun   **Noun**   **Noun**

Adjective   **Adjective**   **Adjective:**

Noun   **Noun**

Adjective   **Adjective**

3 Dimensional shapes or volumes:
Write the noun and adjective under each shape

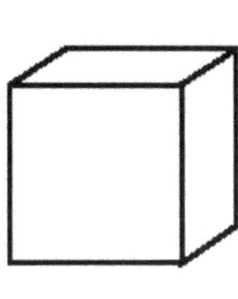 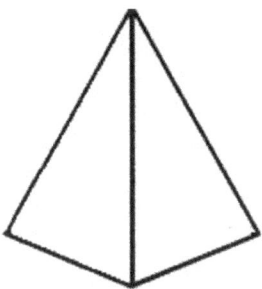 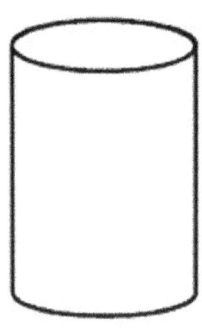

Noun **Noun** **Noun**

Adjective **Adjective** **Adjective**

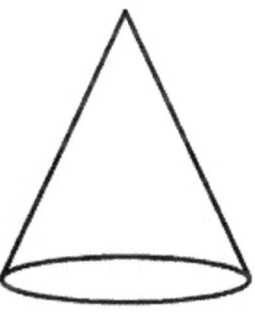 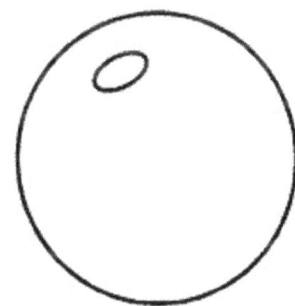

Noun **Noun**

Adjective **Adjective**

Printables 2

roller skates	hat
slippers	rug
chopsticks	belt
electric fan	sunglasses

toothpick	coffee table
cigarette lighter	coat hanger
broom	hair brush
watch	wallet
toilet seat	umbrella

toothbrush	alarm clock
camera	luxury bed
scarf	toy bear
lamp	cup
knife and fork	gloves

Describing Objects
Teacher's Notes

As a teacher, this is one class you have to prepare for and bring the following extras into the class with you:

1: A few examples of colour that you can show to your class for vocabulary; magazines are the easiest resources:
Turquoise, lemon yellow, yellow ochre, crimson, burgundy, lime-green are always easy to find.

2: Some small objects to use for the second guessing game. Try and find about ten, though you won't have time to do all of them:
a CD, roll of tape, scissors, lighter, calculator, wooden spoon or spatula from the kitchen, a key, watch, clear plastic set square, kitchen sponge or scourer are examples.

3: A black bag you can't see through for your objects.

4: Definitely print off the flash cards found in the printables section.

Alternative to Guessing Game 2
Place two chairs facing the white board.
Pick two students to sit in the chairs.
Get one of the remaining students to take an object from the bag. They should not look in the bag otherwise they will see all of the other things.
Each student can use the vocabulary on the white board to describe one thing about the object to the two students sitting up front and pass it on to their class mate.
They cannot mention function including the room the object can be found in.
The students sitting in the chairs can ask questions about the object and guess what it is.
The student to guess first can leave their chair and return to their desk.
Choose another student to take their place at the front of the class room and go through the process again.

Alternative Finish
Get the students to look at the white board for one or two minutes and memorize where the vocabulary is.
Get the students to close their eyes, (no peeking).
Remove one word from the board.
Students open their eyes.
Ask one student to tell them what the missing word is.
Repeat and erase two words.
Repeat and erase three, then four words.

Topic 13: Shopping

You will need to print off and cut out some vocabulary before hand.

Part 4: Daily Life 13

Shopping

Vocabulary and useful stuff

Adjectives and nouns of value:
Extortionate, outrageous
A rip off, expensive, really expensive, an arm and a leg
Dear, overpriced, steep, pricey
Slightly overpriced
Not bad, very reasonable, a bargain, cheap
Next to nothing, cut price, dirt cheap
Free, a give away

Getting things cheaper:
Buy one get one free
Buying in bulk, wholesale
Half price, fifty percent off
On sale, the January sales
End of season shopping
A bargain, to bargain, haggle

Luxury, luxurious, deluxe
Shopaholic
Retail therapy
Supermarket, mall, shopping centre, department store
Green grocers, bakers, butchers
Pharmacy, drug store, chemist

A: Hello to new students   5 minutes
Where is your hometown? What do you do here? Are you a student or do you have a job? Why are you learning English? Which country do you want to go to? Introduce yourself very briefly.

B: Adjectives of Value (*printables*)   15 minutes
Go to the printables and print off the vocabulary. Cut them out.
Prepare, board magnets, Blue Tack or tape.
Hand them to the students, some may get more than one.
Give them one minute to check the words in their dictionaries.
Tell them to stand up and go to the wall or board.
Together, they should stick up their words and make a list on the wall or board, putting them in order. If you have space you can also use the floor for this.

The list should be in order of value; the highest value words at the top and lowest at the bottom.

Afterwards, while they are still standing around the list, answer check and ask one or two students if they would change anything about it? They can move any of the words.

You can also check the meaning of some of the words.

Return to your seats.

C: Discussion

1: BTQ: How often do you go shopping? (past tense)   **10 minutes**
Do you like shopping? Why or why not?
Describe the last time you went shopping. Where did you go? When, who with, what did you buy?

2: Where are the best and worst places to go shopping in town and why?   **10 minutes**
Also a good time to quickly elicit the vocabulary *supermarket, mall, shopping centre, department store, green grocers, bakers, butchers, pharmacy, drug store and chemist* and write them up on the white board.

3: Shopaholics   **10 minutes**
Why do people become addicted to shopping?
Are there any times you lose control when you go shopping? Are there anything's that you just 'had to have'?

4: If you could buy any three luxury items what would they be?   **10 minutes**
Luxury doesn't necessarily mean they are expensive. It also means that they are not essential to us. Also go over the word 'luxurious'.
Answer Check.

Breaktime (5 minutes)

5: Getting it cheaper   **15 minutes**
Think of and describe four ways to get your shopping cheaper, for example, buy in bulk. Answer check and write the answers on the white board.

6: Describe shopping of the future (future tense)   **10 minutes**
Emphasize that this is the future tense and ask students to give examples of usage before they start.

D: Devil's Advocate

Online shopping is not as good as 'real shopping'.   **10 minutes**

E: Role Play:

Buy a briefcase for your boss   **20 minutes**

Draw a simple open briefcase design on the white board while they are doing the Devil's Advocate.

Before the role play go around the class and ask them for any vocabulary that they know for a briefcase for example, *handle, hinges, lining, combination lock and pockets.*
Write the new words with the drawing.

Part 1:   (10 minutes)

<u>Person A:</u> You need to buy a briefcase for your boss's birthday. Everyone in the office has given you money.
<u>Person B:</u> Shop assistant. You sell luxury briefcases. Sell your most expensive one from Europe. Why is it so great?

Part 2:   (10 minutes)

Write this on the white board while they are doing part 1
<u>Person A:</u> When you gave the briefcase to your boss it broke. This is very embarrassing. Your colleagues are all angry with you. Return to the shop and <u>demand</u> your money back.
<u>Person B:</u> Refuse to return the money. Make excuses not to return the money.

F: Drilling the vocabulary and finish

Shopping - Additional Questions and Activities

1: What advice could you give to a Westerner who has never been shopping in China before? Think of three tips. Answer Check   **10 minutes**

2: Think three things you should do when bargaining over something?   **10 minutes**
What are your special ways to '<u>knock down</u>' the price? In China, walking away like you are not interested any more will always get the price of something immediately reduced. Answer Check

3: BTQ: Describe the last gift you bought for someone (past tense)   **10 minutes**
(T12: Describing Objects)
Who for? What occasion was it? When did you buy it? Why did you choose it? Where did you buy it from?

Describe the last gift you received from someone. Who gave it to you and when? Did you like it? Why did they give it to you?

4: Describe the most expensive thing you ever bought? (past tense)   **10 minutes**
(T15: Banks & Money)
When did you buy it and why? Why didn't you buy a cheaper one?

Devil's Advocate

Online shopping will eventually replace 'real' shopping. **10 minutes**

It's great going to the shopping centre at the weekend. **10 minutes**

Girls: Men should accompany their girlfriend or wife when they are shopping
10 minutes

Guys: Women spend far too long shopping. **10 minutes**
Women should spend more time with their husband or boyfriend and do interesting things together.

You need an equal number of male and female students for this, or you could also one of the guys up against two girls or visa versa if you think they are up to the challenge.

Role Play

Shopping Trolley (UK), shopping cart (US) **5 minutes**
A good filler at the end of the lesson if you have an extra few minutes spare.
Person A: You have a lot of shopping. You need to take your shopping trolley outside to the car.
Person B: Security Guard. No one is allowed to take their trolley outside. They have to carry their bags.

Wrong Change **5 minutes**
Person A: Customer. You just bought something for 40RMB with a 100RMB note. You only got 10RMB change. They are 50RMB short. Return to the shop and demand your change. This happened to your friend the other day in the same shop.
Person B: Cashier. Absolutely no way! They left the shop.

Small Supermarket **5 minutes**
Person A: Owner. You have owned a small supermarket for some years. However, a new one has been built nearby. It is very modern. Ask your manager to think of some ideas to attract more customers.
Person B: Manager. Impress your boss with your ideas.

9.9RMB Shop **10 minutes**
A 9.9 RMB shop is the cheapest shop there is. In the UK we have the 'one pound shop'.
Person A: Show owner. You have just opened a 9.9RMB shop. Stand outside and make people come in and buy something. Why are your goods worth buying?
Person B: Passer-by. You are not interested in low quality goods.

Shopping
Printables

Extortionate

Outrageous

A rip off

Expensive

Really Expensive

An arm and a leg

Dear

Overpriced

Steep

Pricey

Slightly overpriced

Not bad

Very reasonable

A bargain

Cheap

Next to nothing

Cut price

Dirt Cheap

Free

A give away

Topic 14
Clothes & Fashion

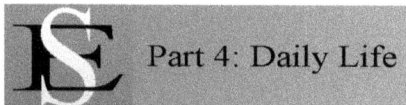 Part 4: Daily Life 14

Clothes & Fashion

Vocabulary and useful stuff

Accessory
Shirt, blouse
Hoody
Jumper, polar-neck
Pants (US), trousers (UK)
Underwear: pants (UK), boxers, knickers
Collar, cuffs
Short and long sleeves
Above the knee, knee length, below the knee
Shoes
Heels, stiletto, wedges, platforms
Arch, sole, toe, laces, insole, tongue

Adjectives to describe clothes (*teacher's notes*)

A: Hello to new students   5 minutes
Where is your hometown? What do you do here? Are you a student or do you have a job? Why are you learning English? Which country do you want to go to? Introduce yourself very briefly. .

B: Pronunciation: 'Clothes'   5 minutes
Many of your students will not be able to say the word 'clothes' properly. The problem comes with the last two sounds 'th' /ð/ and 's' /z/.
Some may pronounce the 'e' to make the word 'clothe es'.
Seeing as this is the name of the topic, its hard to go on without working on this problem, especially if they have a spoken English exam coming up.
Go round each student and check their pronunciation. Drill it a few times.

C: Brainstorm (*teacher's notes*)   10 minutes
All students will know the basics such as hat, t-shirt, coat, jacket, 'pants', socks and shoes.
Ask one student to tell you five things we wear on our head.
Ask one student to tell you five things we wear down to the waist
Ask one student to tell you five things we wear from our waist to the ground.
They may not know these: *Shirt, blouse, hoody, jumper, pants (US), trousers (UK), underwear, pants (UK), boxers, knickers, collar, cuffs, short and long sleeves*. Write words they don't know on the white board.
Ask one student to tell you five things we wear a pair of.

D: Discussion

1: Describe your favourite clothes.   **10 minutes**
Which ones are the most fashionable? Describe them.
Are there any clothes you have that you never wear? Why did you buy them?

2: A romantic date   **10 minutes**
If you were going on a romantic date on a summer's afternoon to the lake or park what would you wear?
If you were going on a romantic date to a great restaurant one evening what would you wear?

3: Why do people wear black?   **5 minutes**
   Why do people wear white and when?
   Which is most suited to you, black or white?

4: BTQ: **When was the last time you bought something new to wear?** (past tense)
What did you buy, who did you go with, where did you go and how much was it?
           10 minutes

Breaktime (5 minutes)
Draw some shoes on the white board ready for the last role play. Alternatively, print off the shoes vocabulary and have that ready.

5: Adjectives to describe clothes (*teacher's notes*)   **10 minutes**
Think of three adjectives to describe clothes.
Answer Check: Write them up on the board and add a couple of your own.
Talk about what accessories are and make a quick list on the board.

6: If you looked like Angelina Jolie or 007 would you like to be a <u>cat-walk</u> model?
Why or why not?   **5 minutes**

E: Devil's Advocate

It is not ok to wear fur   **10 minutes**
Very briefly go over what 'fur' means to the class. Also, which fur most commonly used in clothing. Talk about 'fake fur'

F: Role Play:

Fashion Design   **15 minutes**
(*printables 1*)
Aside from your list of adjectives from Q5, for all role plays either write a list of useful words they can use on the board during the Devil's Advocate or go to the printables and print off the sheet on fashion design. This has some simple vocabulary prompts that your students will find useful. Give them 2-3 minutes to have a look at it.

Person A: You are a famous fashion designer. Talk about your new seasonal designs for men and women the next summer on CCTV.
Person B: CCTV interviewer. This is very exciting. Continually ask follow up questions.

Buy some shoes (*printables 2*) **20 minutes**
You need to have drawn a pair of shoes on the white board at break. You can also give them the handout on shoe vocabulary. Go through this with them for five minutes. If it's with a drawing on the board ask them to label it. If it is from the worksheet then answer check.

Part 1: (10 minutes)
Person A: Customer. You want to buy some shoes. Tell your requirements to the shop assistant and ask for their help.
Person B: Shop assistant. Recommend something to the customer.

Part 2: (5 minutes)
Person A: Customer. Your shoes broke. It was very embarrassing and you hurt your foot. Return to the shop and get your money back.
Person B: Shop assistant. Make excuses not to return the money.

G: Drilling the vocabulary and finish

Clothes & Fashion
Additional Questions and Activities

1: Think of four ways you can use the word 'cool'.   **10 minutes**
(T2: Personality)
Cool can describe someone's appearance, personality, something like a party or concert and also used in place of saying 'ok'. Chinese people say 'xing xing xing' instead of 'ok', for example, when on the phone. We use 'cool' in the same way.
Use of the word 'uncool', for example, when people wear sunglasses on the subway or for some antisocial behaviour.
Answer Check

2: Craze   **10 minutes**
'A popular or widespread fad, fashion that may not last very long.'
Fashion isn't all about clothes. Spend a few minutes giving the class some examples of what a craze is, for example, *Rubix Cubes, the yo-yo, skateboarding, terrible hair styles like 'the mullet'.*
Describe some crazes that you can remember. Where you interested in them and why?

3: Cars   **10 minutes**
Which car would you most like to have? What <u>statement</u> would it make about you?
Again, fashion doesn't have to be about clothes.
Example: A jeep tells people you are a tough and assertive outdoor person. Maybe you could say practical if you use it out of town.

4: Describe this year's fashion.   **10 minutes**
Is it better than last years? Why?
Only use this in a very active class. Students may often find this question surprisingly difficult and it can make a class go quiet very quickly. Try groups of three for this.

5: High heels   **10 minutes**
Women: Do you wear high heels? If not, why not? If yes, when do you where them? Can you wear them all day?
Men: Do you prefer women in high heels or flat shoes? Do you think women should wear high heels at all?

6: Quality   **10 minutes**
When you buy clothes how can you tell their quality?
Stitching, double and single stitching, neat and small stitches, shrink, fade, material.

7: Brand names: **10 minutes**
Think of five different brand names.
Women: Do you buy any brand names? Why or why not?
      Do you prefer to buy <u>fake</u> brand names or the real thing?
Men: Would you buy a fake or real brand name for your girlfriend or wife? Why?

8: Men and Long Hair   **5 minutes**
(T4: Personal Appearance)
Guys: Would you like to grow your hair long? Why or why not?
Girls: Would you like it if your boyfriend had long hair? Why or why not?

9: What kind of person are you?   **5 minutes**
Do you spend time thinking about what you wear? Do you wear similar clothes every day? Are you lazy?

Devil's Advocate

People dress far too casually at work these days with t-shirts, jeans and sports shoes.
Staff should take pride in their company and therefore their appearance.
(T4 Personal Appearance)   **10 minutes**

I love fashion magazines.   **10 minutes**
They are very interesting. We need fashion magazines!

Fashion has gone too far these days.
We must be more conservative about how we dress.   **10 minutes**

If you are lucky enough to have an equal number of girls and guys then use these to really get them arguing.

Guys' argument: Women spend far too long on their appearance.   **10 minutes**
Women should look natural in order to look good.

Guys' argument: Women spend far too long shopping.   **10 minutes**
Women should spend more time with their husband or boyfriend and do interesting things together.

Girls' argument: Men are generally lazy.   **10 minutes**
They should spend more time on their appearance.

Girls: Men should accompany their girlfriend or wife when they are shopping.
                                                                  10 minutes
Of course you need an equal number of male and female students for this, or you could also one of the guys up against two girls if you think they are up to the challenge.

Role Play:

Changing uniforms (*printables 1*)   **10 minutes**
Use the handout on fashion design found in the printables, or write some key words from it up on the white board.

Person A: You are a famous fashion designer. The government has asked you to change the men and women's uniforms for the Beijing subway. Talk about the changes you will make on CCTV.
Person B: CCTV interviewer. This is very exciting. Continually ask follow up questions.

Fashion Design student (*printables 1*)   **10 minutes**
Use the handout on fashion design found in the printables, or write some key words from it up on the white board.
Person A: Student. Attend an interview for a Masters Degree in Fashion Design. Talk about your work. Why are you such a great designer?
Person B: Professor. Ask interview questions. What interests them about the fashion world? Why will their designs be successful in the future?

Image consultant (*teacher's notes*)   **10 minutes**
(*T4: Personal Appearance, printables 2*)
Person A: You are 50 years old. You are still not married and have never had a girlfriend or boyfriend. You have a date this weekend. It's really important. Go and visit an image consultant and ask for advice on changing your appearance.

Person B: Image consultant. Give advice on how this person can change the way they look. Think about hair style, clothes, shoes and also maybe there is something with their behaviour that need changing.

Image consultant alternative: You are going on a business trip to Shanghai for one week. Ask a consultant to help you with formal, informal clothing, daytime and evening clothing.

Holiday with the Grandparents (*teacher's notes*)   **10 minutes**
(*T4: Personal Appearance, printables 3*)
Person A: You will be going on holiday for two weeks with your grandparent next week. Give them advice on improving their appearance. They always wear the same dull brown old clothes. Recommend some bright new, younger looking clothes. Maybe they could change their hair.
Person B: Grandparent. Strongly disagree and be stubborn. You like your clothes; they are familiar and comfortable. Refuse to change the way you look.

Clothes & Fashion
Printables 1

casual formal WOMEN'S MEN'S

Seasonal **Pattern** material

Summer **stripes** man made

Winter **spots** natural

Spring **floral**

Autumn sports

elegant FASHION

DESIGN matching

colours pastel light & dark bright

hot black & white

sexy accessory

Clothes & Fashion
Printables 2

Vocabulary for shoes

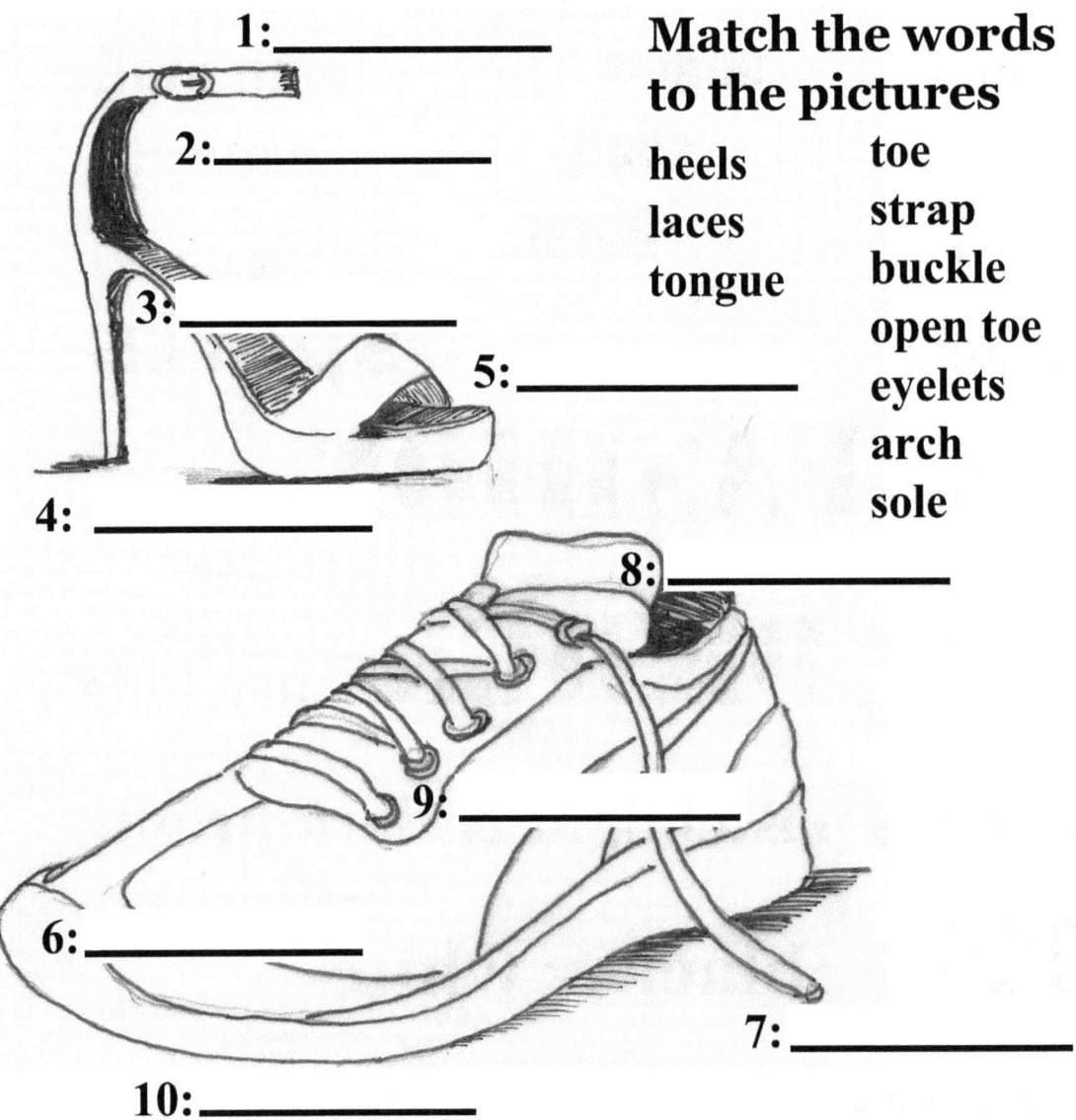

1:_____
2:_____
3:_____
4:_____
5:_____
6:_____
7:_____
8:_____
9:_____
10:_____

Match the words to the pictures

heels   toe
laces   strap
tongue buckle
        open toe
        eyelets
        arch
        sole

Clothes & Fashion
Teacher's Notes

Adjectives to describe clothes
Think of three adjectives to describe clothes.
Students will find this more difficult than most adjectives. The list of these adjectives is absolutely huge one, however and takes up pages. Here are a few of the most useful.

backless
baggy
casual
clingy
comfortable
conservative
cool
designer
-fitting: used with some adjectives and adverbs to make adjectives describing how clothing fits someone, for example, tight/close/loose fitting
formal
hooded
long
low-cut/a low neckline
one-piece
open-necked: clothing where the top button is not fastened
plunging: where a dress shows a lot of the top part of a woman's breasts
polo-neck
revealing
roomy
sensible
skimpy
skin-tight
sleeveless
sporty
straight
strapless
stretchy
tailored
zip up
V-necked

Topic 15: Banks & Money

Part 4: Daily Life 15

Banks & Money

Vocabulary and useful stuff

Cash, coins, 'plastic'
Currency
ATM: Automated Teller Machine
Withdraw, take out
Deposit, put in
Transfer
Balance

Credit card account
Debit card account
Savings card account
Interest
In the green, in the red
Overdraft, limit
Direct debit, standing order
Lottery
Pay rise, a raise, pay increase

A: Hello to new students   5 minutes
Where is your hometown? What do you do here? Are you a student or do you have a job? Why are you learning English? Which country do you want to go to? Introduce yourself very briefly.

B: Brainstorm   10 minutes
Make sure you also cover the words in the top part of the vocabulary above.
Currency: Ask one student at a time
Name five places that use the dollar. They can include the Hong King dollar.
What is the currency of your neighbouring country Japan? The Yen.
What is the currency of your neighbouring country South Korea? The Won.
What is the currency of your neighbouring country Mongolia? Tugrik.
What is the currency of France? The Euro. It used to be the Franc.
What is the currency of the UK?
ATM's
What does ATM stand for?
Ask one student to tell you four functions of an ATM.

C: Discussion

1: Bank Accounts (*teacher's notes*)　　　　　　　　　　　　　　　**15 minutes**
Write these three clearly in a list on the left hand side of the white board.
Credit card account
Debit card account
Savings account

What is the difference between a credit card and a debit account?　　(5 minutes)
Most students won't know, so tell them if they don't know to have a guess and that you will be explaining it together in two minutes.
Draw simple graphs to explain it. These can be found in the teacher's notes.

2: Do you use a credit card? Why or why not?　　　　　　　　　　**10 minutes**
If you don't have one would you use one in the future?
What are the advantages and disadvantages of using a credit card?

3: When you were a child how much pocket money did you get?　　**5 minutes**
What did you spend it on? (past tense)

4: Describe the most expensive thing you ever bought? (past tense)　　**10 minutes**
(T13: Shopping)
When did you buy it and why? Why didn't you buy a cheaper one?

Breaktime (5 minutes)

5: Found a Wallet　　　　　　　　　　　　　　　　　　　　　　**10 minutes**
If you found a wallet with 3000 RMB and credit cards what would you do and why?

6: If you won 100 million RMB on the <u>lottery</u> what would you spend it on?
(T 17: Numbers & Quantities)　　　　　　　　　　　　　　　　　　**10 minutes**
Do you ever play the lottery? Why or why not? What is your opinion of playing the lottery?

D: Devil's Advocate

You should never lend anyone your money.　　　　　　　　　　　**10 minutes**

E: Role Play:

Negotiate a <u>pay rise</u> with your boss.　　　　　　　　　　　　　**10 minutes**
<u>Person A:</u> Everyone in the office has had a pay rise except you. You think you work just as hard as everyone else. Go and ask your boss why?
<u>Person B:</u> Boss. Give an explanation and refuse to give them any more money.

Borrow some money from an old friend (*T7: Friends, printables 1*) **20 minutes**
If you have recently done this activity in T7: Friends then use another roleplay from the alternative questions and activities.

Part 1: Small Talk (5 minutes)
Before you start tell the class that if you are Person A you must make 'small talk' before they ask for the money. Write it on the board and ask the class what they think it means: *talk about their family, you heard they had a baby, you heard that they got promoted, you heard that they bought a new car or talk about the weather.*
Tell them that Person A must make small talk for at least 2 minutes before asking for the money.

Part 2: (10 minutes)
Person A: You really need some money. You asked the bank but they said no. However, you heard that recently an old friend won a lot of money on the 'lottery'. Give them a call and ask if you can borrow some. Never give up. You need this money! Make small talk first.
Person B: You haven't heard from this person in five years; no e-mails; no calls or even any text messages. Why should you lend them any money?

Part 3: (5 minutes)
While they are doing part one, quickly write this up on the white board.
Person A: You kindly leant your friend the money but after six months you really need it back. Ask for it back.
Person B: Make excuses not to return it.

F: Drilling the vocabulary and finish

Banks & Money
Additional Questions and Activities

1: Think of three 'quick-fix' ways to get money if you had a serious debt to pay off quickly. **5 minutes**

2: If you could buy any three luxury items what would they be? **10 minutes**
(T13: Shopping)
Luxury doesn't necessarily mean they are expensive. It also means that they are not essential to us. Also go over the word 'luxurious'.

3: Do you overspend or are you frugal with your money? **10 minutes**
Do you save money or are you impulsive? Give an example.

4: What is the most important to you in a partner?   10 minutes
Money, Appearance or Love? Why? (T8: Romance & Dating)
Students have to rate each one using percentages, for example, *'Love 60%, Appearance 20% and Money 20%.*
Some may change the question if they want, for example, by adding personality. This is ok. It is their discussion to do with it what they want.
Answer check.

Devil's Advocate

Gambling should be made legal.   10 minutes

Men should pay for everything on a date!   10 minutes
You really need a class with equal number of male and female students for this.
It's also possible to put one male student against three girls or visa versa if their English is pretty good or they are very outspoken and love arguing. It's a matter of getting to know your students.

Going into business with a friend is a terrible idea.   10 minutes

Roleplay

Pocket Money   5 minutes
Person A: Child under 12. All your friends get more pocket money than you. Ask your parents for more money. Don't stop. Be persistent.
Parent B: Parents. No way! You think they already get enough. Give examples of how you already spoil them and why you shouldn't give them any more.

Wrong Change   10 minutes
Person A: Customer. You just bought something for 40RMB with a 100RMB note. You only got 10RMB change. They are 50RMB short. Return to the shop and demand your change. This happened to your friend the other day.
Person B: Cashier. Absolutely no way! They left the shop.

Go into business with a friend   10 minutes
(T7 Friends)
Person A: You want to turn your hobby into a business. Persuade your friend to join you.
Person B: You don't think it's a good idea. Think of reasons to say no.

Paying the Bill 10 minutes
Person A: You are in a restaurant and it's time to pay for the bill. Unfortunately you forgot your wallet. Ask your friend if they can pay for you.
Person B: Refuse to help. Your friend always forgets their wallet and never pays. They borrowed 100 RMB from you last week and didn't pay you back.

Negotiating for a computer contract (*printables*) 15 minutes

Spend five minutes explaining this to the class.
This is for more advanced students. Go through some of the things that you would consider, if you were trying to promote your services while negotiating for a contract.
This can be for two or three students. For two students simply use Person A and Person B.

Person A: You are the boss of a new company. You have just opened a new office.
You need a company to help you install 100 new computers.
You want the price to be 500 RMB for each computer installed.
That will be 50,000 RMB in total.
Also you need the job done quickly. Your offices will open in two weeks.
You know many other companies that can do it at a cheaper price.

Person B: Your company will do the job but your boss wants you to do it for 650 RMB for each computer. This will be 65,000 RMB in total.
Although it is more expensive your company is one of the best in town. It is well-known for its professional service.
WHAT EXCELLENT SERVICES DO YOU OFFER?
Impress your boss. YOU MUST GET THIS CONTRACT.

Person C: Your company will do the job but your boss only wants you to do it for 550 RMB for each computer.
This will be 55,000 RMB in total.
You are a new company in town. You can do it cheaper and faster.
You need the money. YOU MUST GET THIS CONTRACT
Your boss will be angry if you fail.

Debt Collection 5 minutes
Person A: You work at the bank. Your customer owes the bank 100,000 RMB. They have not been making their monthly repayments. Phone them up and ask for the money back.
Person B: Make excuses not to repay the money. Try and negotiate for more time.

Banks & Money - Printables

Roleplay: Negotiating
A: You are the boss of a new company. You have just opened a new office. You need a company to help you <u>install</u> 100 new computers.

You want the price to be 500 RMB for each computer installed.
That will be 50,000 RMB in total.
Also you need the job done quickly. Your offices will open in two weeks.

You know many other companies that can do it at a cheaper price.

Roleplay: Negotiating
B: Your company will do the job but your boss wants you to do it for 650 RMB for each computer. This will be 65,000 RMB in total.

Although it is more expensive your company is one of the best in town. It is well-known for its professional service.
WHAT EXCELLENT SERVICES DO YOU OFFER?

Impress your boss. **YOU MUST GET THIS CONTRACT.**

Roleplay: Negotiating
C: Your company will do the job but your boss only wants you to do it for 550 RMB for each computer.
This will be 55,000 RMB in total.
You are a new company in town. You can do it cheaper and faster.

You need the money. **YOU MUST GET THIS CONTRACT.**
Your boss will be angry if you fail.

Banks & Money
Teacher's Notes

Credit Cards & Debit Cards – Graph

Many students get very confused about the difference between the two cards. Some think they are the same thing. Some assume an arranged overdraft is with happens with a credit card. The best way to clear up such confusion is to draw these simple graphs on the white board to explain credit cards visually.

Credit Card Account:

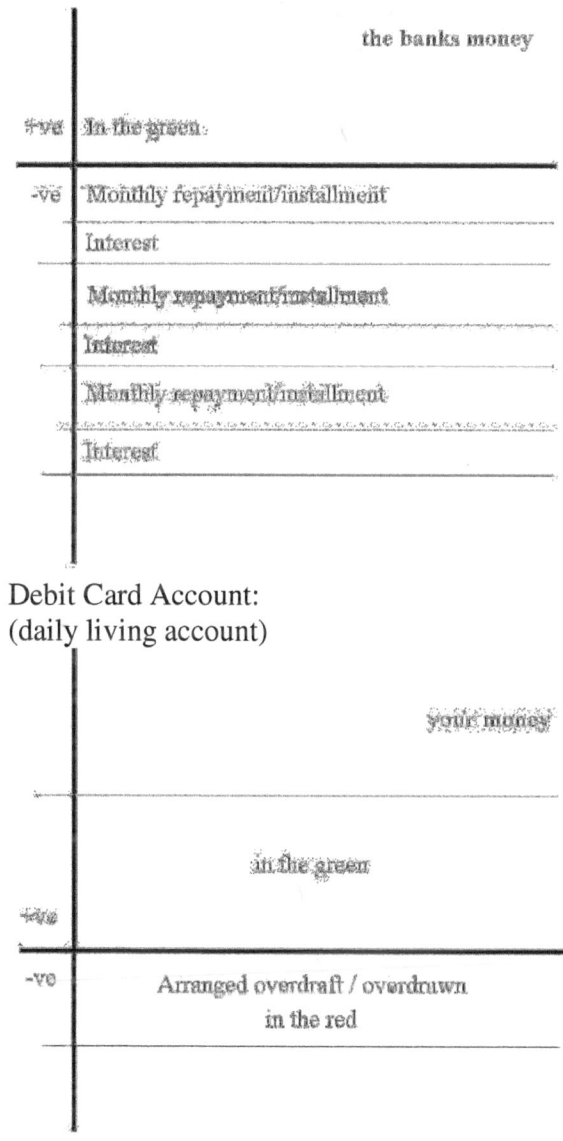

Debit Card Account:
(daily living account)

Topic 16: Giving Directions

A fast moving topic where your students will practice speaking simply and quickly.

Part 4: Daily Life

Giving Directions

Vocabulary and useful stuff

Right, left, go straight ahead/on
Straight over, straight across
Landmarks
Junctions, intersection
Crossroads
Roundabout (UK), traffic circle (US)
Clockwise, anti-clockwise, first exit
T-junction
Traffic lights, red, amber, green
Zebra crossing, cross walk (some parts of US)
Over/under pass
Pedestrian
Pavement (UK), sidewalk (US)

A: Hello to new students   5 minutes
Where is your hometown? What do you do here? Are you a student or do you have a job? Why are you learning English? Which country do you want to go to? Introduce yourself very briefly.

B: Elicit Vocabulary (teacher's notes)   30 minutes
The students will need all the vocabulary in front of them to look at on the board.
Take your time and make it fun.
1: How do you ask for directions?
There are many variations on this but always start with 'Excuse me' and 'please?' Both have a tone that sinks and then rises.

"Excuse me. Could you tell me the way to the museum please?"

Note, 'you' and 'to the' becomes 'yu' / y ə / and 'tu thu' / t ə ð ə / forming connected speech. Also, if we say "Could you <u>please</u> tell me" the meaning changes to irritation or begging (see Appendix B: Using Phonetics).

2: What is the most important information we need to know when giving directions? Elicit all the vocabulary above using diagrams drawn on the white board to help explain things, (*landmarks, road features, and turnings*).

C: Exercise 1: Drilling   10 minutes
Map 1: Draw this quickly on the whiteboard.

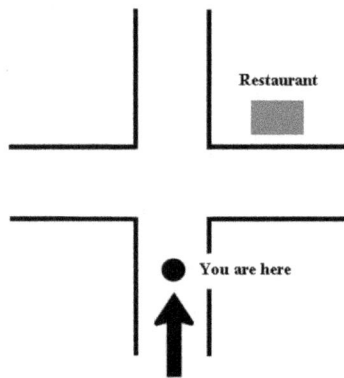

1: Give your students one minute to work out how to get to the restaurant.
2: Ask each student.
3: Now give them the simplest directions you have. In the UK we don't normally use north, south, east or west to help us. In real life someone may point with their arm out to show us the direction "Go down there….." Write it on the board:

'Go down there
tu thu crossroads
turn right
an it's on your left.'

Note: In spoken English 'and' becomes 'an'. Remember that 'to' becomes 'tu' / t ə / and 'the' becomes 'thu' / ð ə /. This allows us to say the sentence much faster.

4: This takes no more than two seconds to say. Drill it and go around each student and get them to say it quickly and clearly. Make them do it again if they get tongue-tied.

C: Exercise 2: Drilling   10 minutes
Map2: Now add to your map and move the restaurant and repeat the process from Map1.

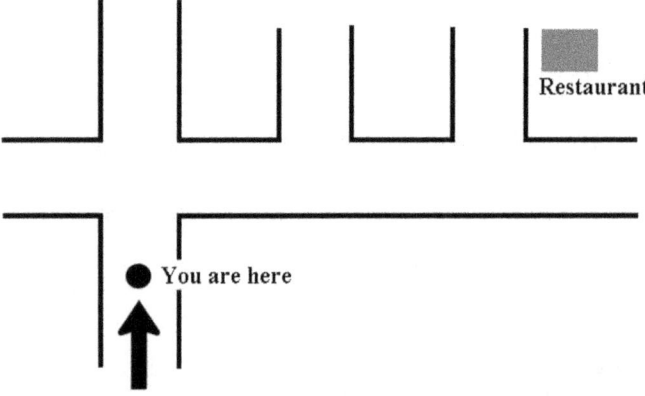

Give them two minutes to work this one out. Encourage them to practice vocally.
Go down there, tu thu crossroads, turn right, third left an it's on your right.
(Note: we do not need to say "go third left, take the third left" or "turn third left")

Breaktime (5 minutes)

An Additional 10 minutes has been left in the second half of the lesson so you don't have to rush your activities. The total time for the second half of the lesson is 50 minutes. If you have spare time a quick role play can be added at the end as a filler.

D: Exercise 3: Worksheet (*printables part 1*)   10 minutes

Print off the map found in the printables section.
Students work in pairs to complete the answers. Don't wait until everyone has finished. Make sure you keep an eye on the time.
Answer Check

Explain that sometimes people use 'blocks' to give directions, for example, "go down two blocks"

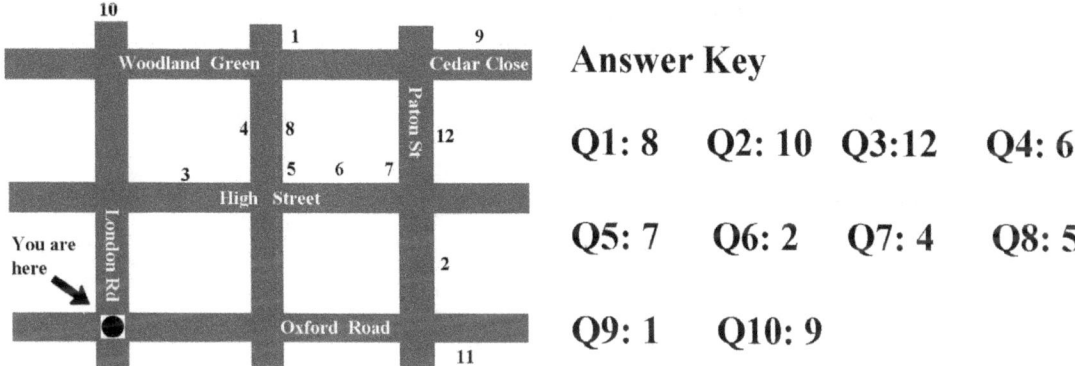

Answer Key

Q1: 8   Q2: 10   Q3: 12   Q4: 6

Q5: 7   Q6: 2   Q7: 4   Q8: 5

Q9: 1   Q10: 9

E: Exercise 4: Worksheet (*printables part 2*)   15 minutes

If you go to the printables you will find two maps, Map A and Map B. You will notice that they are of the same area but they have different places marked on each one.

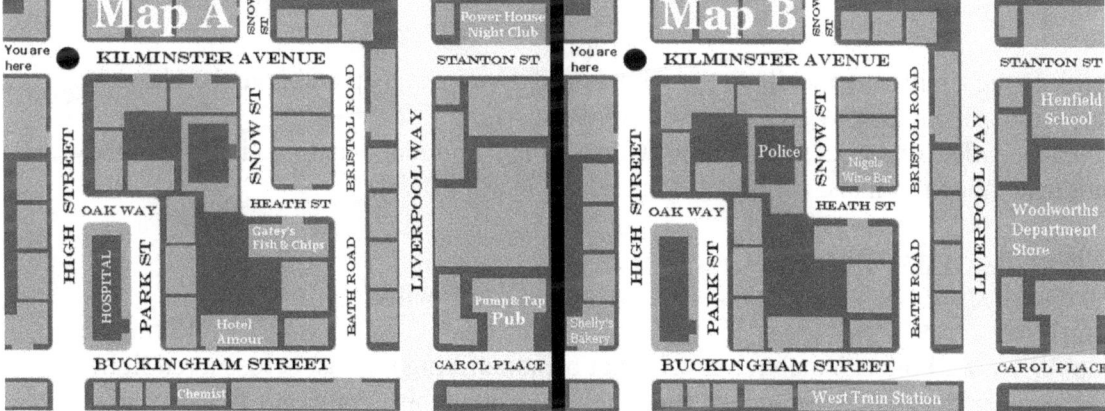

Put students into pairs. Give one student Map A and the other Map B. They should make sure that their partner can't see each other's maps.
Starting at the same place marked 'You are here', each student should then take turns asking for directions for the places written at the top of the paper. These will be marked on their classmates map but not their own, for example,

Map A student *"Excuse me. Could you tell me the way to the police station please?"*
This will be marked on their partner's map. The Map B student should give their partner directions, who should follow the instructions and try and find the right place.

F: Roleplay

Asking for directions on the phone (*printables part 3*)   **15 minutes**

Print off the worksheet found in the printables section. The locations from Exercise 4 are now put together on the same map with a few additions. The starting point has been changed. The students need to find the GLC Offices on the left hand side of the map.

Person A: You have an important job interview today at the GLC Offices. Your taxi driver has dropped you at the wrong place 'You are here'.
Phone the office and ask for directions. You are lost and very confused. Continually ask the receptionist questions. Make it difficult for them.
Person B: Receptionist. Politely give them directions.

Swap roles and change the drop off point 'You are here' to a different location.

G: Exercise 5: Drilling   10 minutes

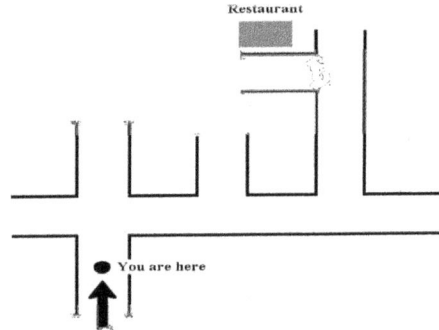

Go back to the simple map work on the whiteboard. Draw the map and give the class two minutes to work out how to give directions to the restaurant.
Go to each student and ask for directions. Correct them and make them do it again if they are not fast enough or make a mistake. Make them work!

H: Filler Activity: Roleplay

If you have a spare few minutes this is a good one to finish with.
Bad Driving   (5 minutes)
Person A: Traffic Police. You have caught that person driving too fast across a red light. Your computer says this is the second time they have done this. You don't like drivers who drive too fast. Give them a heavy fine.
Person B: Driver. Make an excuse. Avoid paying the fine.

I: Drilling the vocabulary and finish

Giving Directions
Printables 1

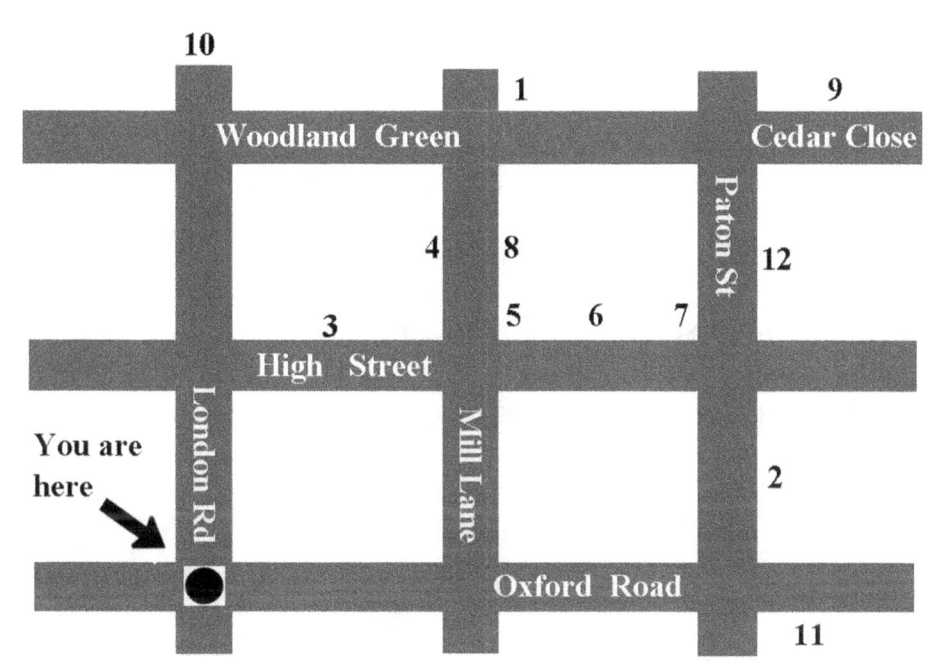

8 - 1: Go down Oxford Road and turn left at Mill Lane. Go down one block to the crossroads. Go straight over and it's the second building in your right.

___**2:** Go straight down London Road to the second crossroads. Go straight over Woodland Green and it's directly in front of you.

___**3:** Go down London Road to the first crossroads. Turn right down the High Street. Keep going all the way to Paton Street. Turn left at the crossroads and it's on your right.

___**4:** Go down Oxford Street to Paton Street. Go left down one block to the High Street. Turn left at the crossroads and it's the second building on your right.

___**5:** Go down London Road to the High Street. Turn right and go down two blocks to the crossroads at Paton Street and it's on the first corner on your left.

___**6:** Go down London Road two blocks to Woodland Green and turn right. Go down another two blocks to the crossroads before Cedar Close then turn right. Go straight over the first crossroads on Paton Street and it's on your left.

___**7:** Go straight down Oxford Road to the crossroads on Mill Lane. Turn left until you get to High Street. Go straight over and it's on your left.

___**8:** Go down London Road to High Street. When you get there take a right. When you reach Mill Lane you will see it opposite you on the left hand corner of the crossroads.

___**9:** Go all the way down Oxford Road two blocks until you reach Paton Street. Turn left and then left again down High Street. At the first crossroads go right to Woodland Green. When you get there you will see it opposite you on the right.

___**10:** Go straight down London Road to Woodland Green. Turn right and go down two blocks until you reach Cedar Close. It's on your left down Cedar Close.

Giving Directions
Printables 2

Map A:

Ask your classmate for directions.

"Excuse me. Could you tell me the way to the _____ please?

These places are not on your map. They are on Map B

1: School   **2: Department store**   **3: The train station**

4: Bakery   **5: The wine bar**   **6: Police station**

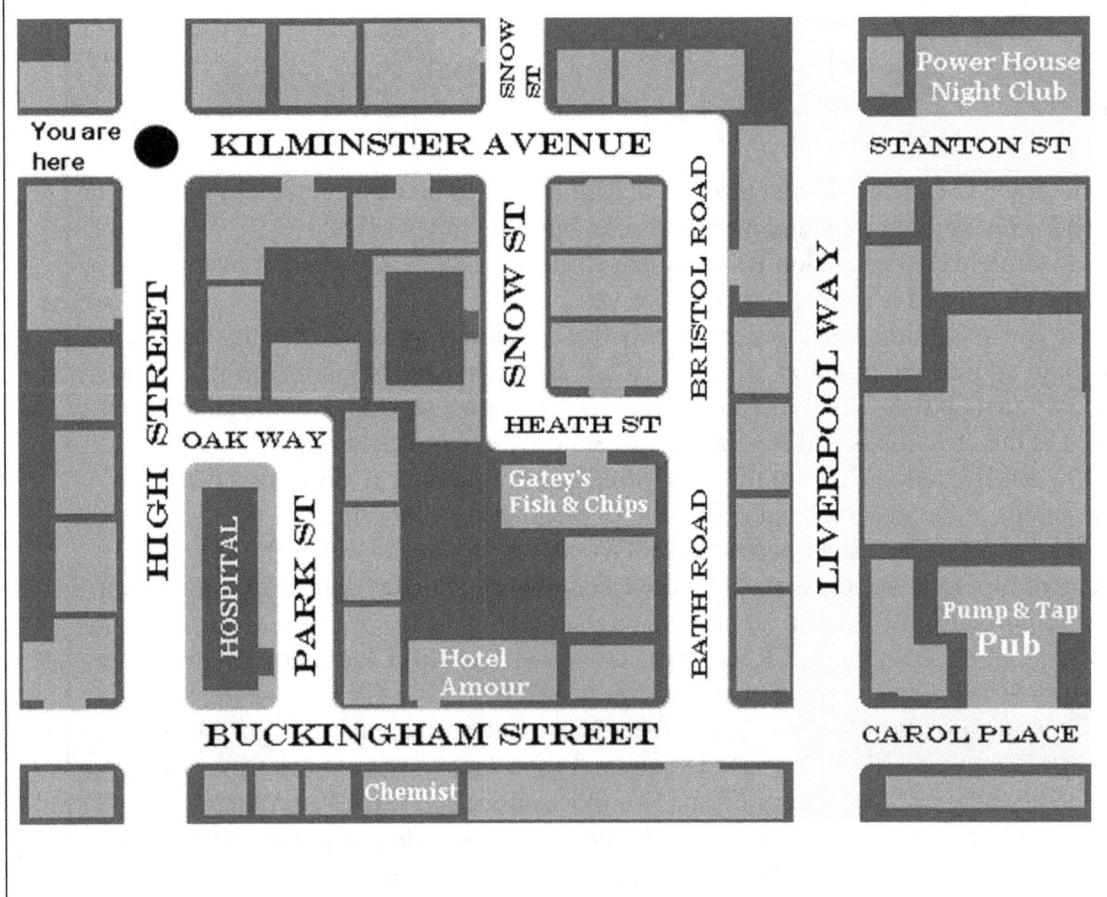

Map B:

Ask your classmate for directions.

"Excuse me. Could you tell me the way to the _____ please?

These places are not on your map. They are on Map A

1: Hospital   2: Night Club   3: Fish & chip shop

4: Hotel   5: Chemist   6: Pub

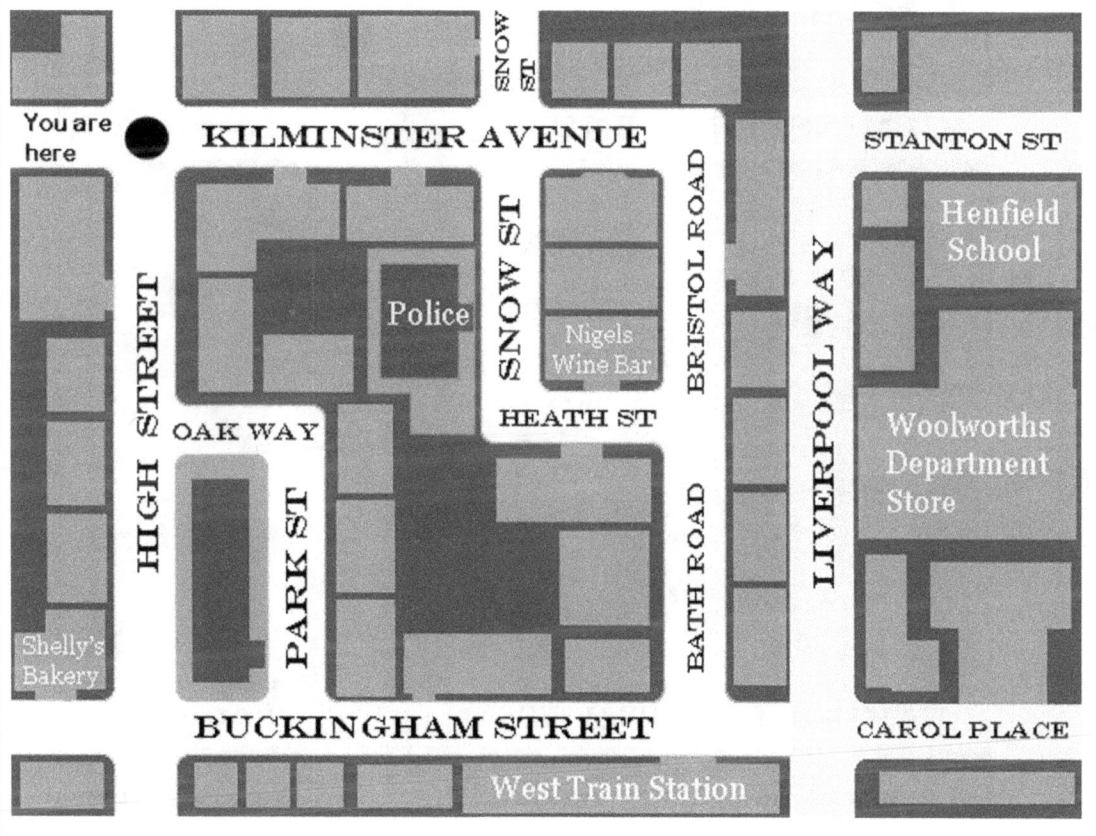

Giving Directions
Printables 3

Person A:
You have an important job interview today at the GLC Offices.

Your taxi driver has dropped you at the wrong place **"You are here"**.

Phone the office and ask for directions. You are lost and very confused. **Continually ask the receptionist questions. Make it difficult for them.**

Person B:
Receptionist. Politely give them directions.

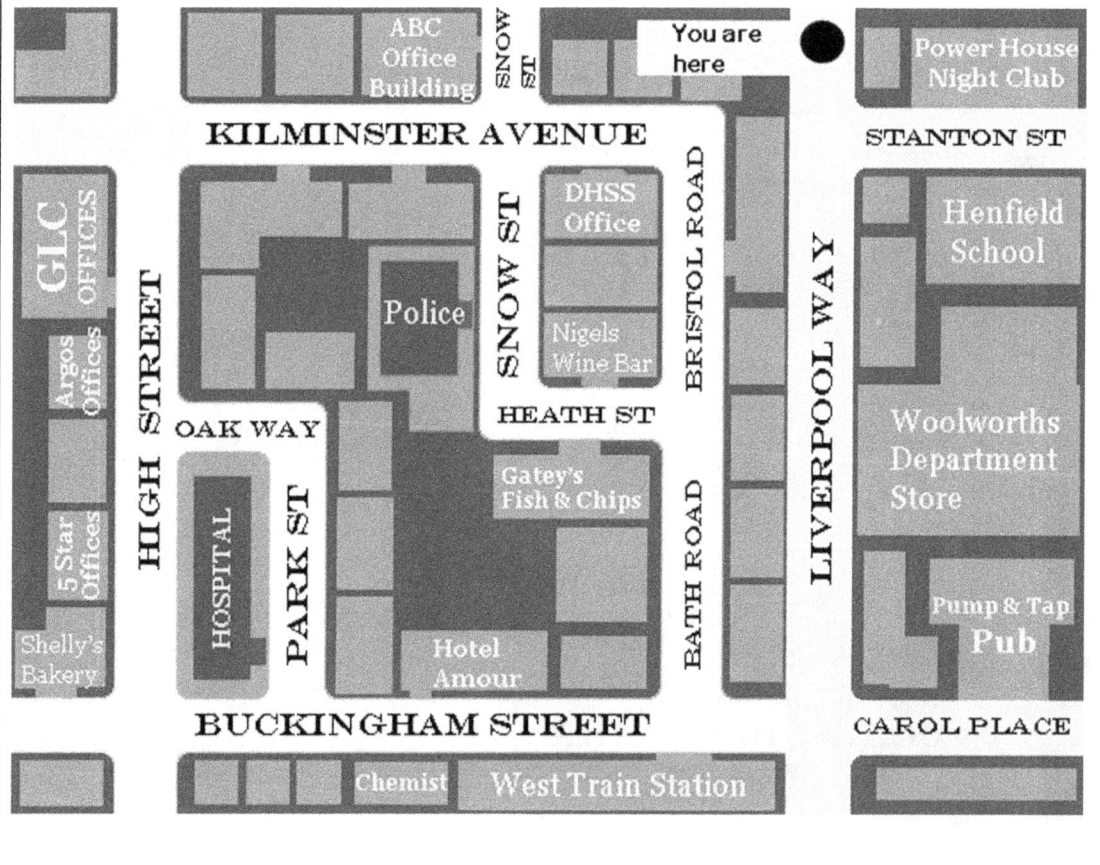

Giving Directions
Teacher's Notes

Aims
When someone gives you directions, often they will be busy and may not have much time. Information is normally given in the quickest and most simple manner possible so that they can continue on their way.

This lesson focuses on speaking quickly and economically with listening also playing a key role.

Repetition and drilling are also important. Make your students work hard during this lesson. If they make a mistake when giving directions make them do it again. If they are too slow make them do it faster.

Open Discussion
This topic differs from others as during the start of the lesson, at least half an hour depends on teacher talk time and eliciting the new vocabulary that is necessary when giving directions. Ask as many questions to the students as possible while giving the new vocabulary so that they are not just listening.

Manage your White Board
Keep your white board as tidy as possible with vocabulary down one side. Allow space for maps, discussion questions and roleplay.

Drawing
For things like junctions and road crossings you will have to do some simple drawings on the white board. You will also need to draw some simple maps as clearly as possible.

Exercises
Another variation from other topics is the use of exercises in the form of maps which should be printed out and given to the students. This will create a 'heads-down' effect for at least 20 minutes during which time you can prepare for the next activity.

Topic 17: Numbers & Quantities

Part 4: Daily Life 17

Numbers & Quantities

Vocabulary and useful stuff (*also go to teacher's notes for detailed information about measurements*)
Math (US), Maths (UK). This is great for pronunciation practice.
On the dot, bang on 10
Around 10, 10ish
Coming up to seven, almost seven
Just past six
Round off the number, a round number
Imperial, metric

A: Hello to new students — 5 minutes
Where is your hometown? What do you do here? Are you a student or do you have a job? Why are you learning English? Which country do you want to go to? Introduce yourself very briefly.

B: Brainstorm — 10 minutes
The number of ways we use numbers and measurements is vast. Ask the students the most common forms of measurement and what we use them to measure, for example, we use kilometres to measure distance. Make a list on the left hand side of the white board.

C: Discussion

1: Basic maths (past tense) — 10 minutes
Did you enjoy maths when you were at school? Why or why not? What part of it did you enjoy or hate the most?
You may get students asking you for vocabulary. Make sure you write it all on the board for the whole class and go through it after discussion.

2: Basic maths: Exercises (*printables*) — 15 minutes
Put students in pairs. Give them the two question sheets, A and B. They should ask each other the questions in spoken English. When they answer they should give the whole answer, for example, "five plus five is/equals ten" not simply "ten"

Go through the spoken English vocabulary with them included at the top of each sheet. Include pronunciation.
+ plus, - minus, x times, / divided by, = is/equals, 0.5 naught/zero point five
½ a half, 1/3 a third, ¼ a quarter, 1/5 a fifth.
For fun ask someone what one less than a million is. Also ask what a billion (9 zeros) and a trillion (12 zeros) means.

Answers Sheet A:
1: 6 + 6 = 36 **2:** 100 − 33 = 67 **3:** 99/ 3 = 33 **4:** 668 x 8 = 5,344 **5:** 10 − 6868 = -6858
Answers Sheet B:
1: 338 + 338 = 676 **2:** 886 − 668 = 218 **3:** 6 / 8 = 0.75 **4:** 77 x 33 = 2,541
5: 10 − 70.6868 = -60.6868

3: BTQ: Distance (*teacher's notes*)   **15 minutes**
Describe your longest journey. How long in time and distance? Who with, when, why did you go on the journey, what transport did you use, did you have to transfer? If you had to transfer, how long was each stage of the journey? (past tense)

Go through distances included in the teacher's notes.

Breaktime (5 minutes)

4: Time   **10 minutes**
Before the discussion in Q5, go through this basic spoken vocabulary with the students. You don't have to draw a clock or anything, just write up the times as numbers. In spoken English we don't often refer to the 24 hr clock.

Q: Think of two ways to say 6.30
   Think of two ways to say 6.15
   Think of two ways to say 6.23
   Think of three ways to say 6.56
   Think of another way to say 6.03

A: 6.30 – six thirty, half past six and often just 'half past' in spoken
   6.15 – six fifteen, quarter past six and often just 'quarter past' in spoken English
   6.23 – We always 'round off' the number to a 'round number' In this case we would
         say 6.25 ('twenny' not 'twenty'). We could also say twenty five past.
   6.56 – Coming up to seven, almost seven, six fifty five, five to'
   6.03 – Just past six

5: Time: Your daily schedule   **10 minutes**
Put students into pairs. They should tell their classmate about their daily schedule. When they normally get up, have breakfast, go out, work or college routine, lunch, evening meal, go home, relax/personal interests, go to bed.
Tell them this is an important listening exercise.

When they have finished get them to change partners, turning to face their neighbour then tell their new partner about their previous partner's schedule. This is now a memory test. Their classmate should ask questions about the previous partner's schedule.

6: Lucky numbers   **10 minutes**
What are the lucky and unlucky numbers in China and what do they mean? Do you have any of these numbers on your phone? Answer Check

D: Devil's Advocate   10 minutes

After school is finished we normally forget most of the maths we learnt. Maths should therefore not be a <u>compulsory</u> subject.

E: Role Play:

Only an acquaintance (T7 *Friends: printables 2*)   **10 minutes**

<u>Person A:</u> You are new in town. You don't have any friends and are lonely. However, yesterday you met someone in a coffee shop and got their telephone number. <u>Phone them up</u> and ask them to join you for lunch sometime. Be persistent. If they are busy think of another time.
<u>Person B:</u> You don't really know this person and regret giving them your telephone number. Make excuses not to meet them.

You are late: **10 minutes**

Part 1:   (5 minutes)
<u>Person A:</u> You have been waiting for your friend for half an hour. Phone them and ask them where they are. They are always late! Mention the time they should have arrived and the reason for you meeting up.
<u>Person B:</u> Make an excuse. You will be there shortly.

Part 2:   (5 minutes)
<u>Person A:</u> After another 15 minutes they still haven't arrived. Phone them again.
<u>Person B:</u> Make another excuse. You will be there shortly.

Teacher: If you have any spare time you can do this a third time.

F: Drilling the vocabulary and finish

Numbers & Quantities
Additional Questions and Activities

1: Time: Are you a good time keeper or are you sometimes late? **5 minutes**
How often?

2: Time: Describe the last time you were late. (past tense) **10 minutes**
Why were you late?

3: Time: If you were a manager, what would you do if an employee was late?
How about for a second and third time? **5 minutes**

4: Temperature **5 minutes**
Think of three verbs we can use when water changes temperature, for example, 'freeze'. Try and think of the nouns that go with them, for example, 'ice'.

5: Temperature (past tense) **10 minutes**
2008 'China's Year'. Talk about what happened across China during January and February of 2008.

6: Speed **5 minutes**
What is the fastest vehicle ever made? (*teacher's notes*)
What is the fastest animal? How fast can it go? How is it able to go so fast?

Answer:
The Voyager 1 Space Probe is going at 57,437 mph (92, 440 kph) and is still going faster having now left our solar system.
The Peregrine Falcon is the fastest animal and dives headfirst down through the sky at over 200mph (321.9 kph).

7: Lottery (T15: Banks & Money) **10 minutes**
Do you play the lottery? Why or why not? What is your opinion of people who play the lottery?
You have a 1: 14 million chance to win the 6 number lottery in the UK. There is a greater chance of being hit by lightning which is about 2.5 million to one.

Roleplay

Bad Driving (T16: Giving Directions) **5 minutes**
Person A: Traffic Police. You have caught that person driving too fast across a red light. Your computer says this is the second time they have done this. You don't like drivers who drive too fast. Give them a heavy fine.
Person B: Driver. Make an excuse. Avoid paying the fine.

Negotiating for a computer contract (*T15: Banks and Money, printables*)　**10 minutes**

This is for more advanced students. Go through some of the things that you would consider, if you were trying to promote your services while negotiating for a contract. This can be for two or three students. For two students simply use Person A and Person B.

Person A: You are the boss of a new company. You have just opened a new office.
You need a company to help you install 100 new computers.
You want the price to be 500 RMB for each computer installed.
That will be 50,000 RMB in total.
Also you need the job done quickly. Your offices will open in two weeks.
You know many other companies that can do it at a cheaper price.

Person B: Your company will do the job but your boss wants you to do it for 650 RMB for each computer. This will be 65,000 RMB in total.
Although it is more expensive your company is one of the best in town. It is well-known for its professional service.
WHAT EXCELLENT SERVICES DO YOU OFFER?
Impress your boss. YOU MUST GET THIS CONTRACT.

Person C: Your company will do the job but your boss only wants you to do it for 550 RMB for each computer.
This will be 55,000 RMB in total.
You are a new company in town. You can do it cheaper and faster.
You need the money. YOU MUST GET THIS CONTRACT
Your boss will be angry if you fail.

Numbers & Quantities
Printables

Basic Maths A:

Spoken English Vocabulary:
+ plus (and), - minus, x times, / divided by, = is/equals, 0.5 naught point five
½ a half, 1/3 a third, ¼ a quarter, 1/5 a fifth

What's five plus five? Ten or you can say **Five plus five is ten/ equals ten**

Questions: Ask these questions to your friend. They can use a <u>calculator</u> to help

1: 6 + 6 =? **2:** 100 – 33 =? **3:** 99/ 3 =? **4:** 668 x 8 =? **5:** 10 – 6868 =?

6: What is their telephone number? They should answer you as fast as possible. They should tell you two times.

Basic Maths B:

Spoken English Vocabulary:
+ plus (and), - minus, x times, / divided by, = is/equals, 0.5 naught point five
½ a half, 1/3 a third, ¼ a quarter, 1/5 a fifth

What's five plus five? Ten or you can say **Five plus five is ten/ equals ten**

Questions: Ask these questions to your friend. They can use a <u>calculator</u> to help

1: 338 + 338 =? **2:** 886 – 668 =? **3:** 6 / 8 =? **4:** 77 x 33 =? **5:** 10 – 70.6868 =?

6: What is their telephone number? They should answer you as fast as possible. They should tell you two times.

Numbers & Quantities
Teacher's Notes

Useful Information: (Imperial/metric)

Distance:
1 mile = 1.609 kilometers
1 mile = 5280 feet
1 foot = 12 inches

The nearest solar system from ours is Proxima Century which is 4.24 light years from the Earth. That's about 5.9 x 10 12 miles, so close to 6 trillion miles.

1 light year = 5,878499981/ six trillion miles (10 trillion kilometres)
At the moment, our fastest vehicle Voyager travelling at 57,437 mph (92, 440 kph) would take 76,000 years to get there.

Speed:
1 mph = 1.609 kph

Fastest vehicle: The Voyager 1 Space Probe is going at 57,437 mph (92, 440 kph) and is still going faster having now left our solar system.
The USA is testing the Falcon HTV-2 which is a plane that can go 13,000mph. That's 20 times the speed of sound, though so far has been unsuccessful.
Fastest animal: In a dive it is the Peregrine Falcon, the fastest bird that dives headfirst down through the sky. They can travel over 200mph, (321.9 kph).
If there were a short running race, the Cheetah would win at 70mph, (112.7 kph).
Speed of sound: (*supersonic, sonic boom*). This is 1,236 kilometres per hour (768 mph).
Speed of light: Light speed is 299,792,458 metres per second (approximately 186,282. miles per second).

Weight:
Metric
1000 kilos (kg) = 1 tonne
1 kilo = 1000 grams

Avoir
1 pound (lb) = 16 ounces (oz)
1 stone = 14 pounds
1 ton (UK) = 2,240 pounds
1 ton (US) = 2,000 pounds
1 Kilogram = 2.205 pounds

Heaviest person: Pauline Potter from Sacramento was entered into the 2012 Guinness Book of Records at 643 lbs. That's 291.7 kilos.
According to Guinness World Records, the heaviest woman ever is Rosalie Bradford, who registered a peak weight of 1,200 lbs. in January 1987. That's 544.3 kilos.
Jon Brower Minnoch was recorded as the heaviest person that ever lived weighing in at 1400 lbs. That's 634 kilos!

Capacity & Volume:
(Imperial/metric)

1 gallon (UK) = 4.546 litres
1 gallon (US) = 3.785 litres
1 gallon = 8 pints

Temperature:
0 °C/Centigrade = 32 (°F) Fahrenheit
Celsius and Centigrade mean the same thing.

Absolute zero is the theoretical lowest possible temperature at minus 273.15 °C.
Coldest inhabited place: Oymyakon is a rural area in the Oymyakonsky District of the Sakha Republic, Russia. It is the coldest permanently inhabited area on Earth.
It has a population of 472 with a record temperature of minus 71 °C.
Verkhoyansk is a town in Sakha Republic with a population of 1,300. Its coldest temperature was minus 69 °C. There, the ink in your pen will freeze, along with axel grease. Your spit will freeze before it hits the ground and plastic bags will crack. Skin sticks to metal and the local school closes if the temperature drops below minus 53 °C.

Topic 18: Food

The additional questions and activities section can also be used for T19: Cooking and T20: Eating Out.

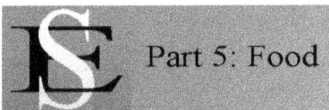 Part 5: Food

Food

Vocabulary and useful stuff

Nutrition, vitamins
Protein, carbs
Diet
Vegetarian, vegan
Dairy products
Pesticides, insecticide
Organic
Antibiotics, steroids, growth hormones
Intensive farming, battery farming

A: Hello to new students — 5 minutes
Where is your hometown? What do you do here? Are you a student or do you have a job? Why are you learning English? Which country do you want to go to? Introduce yourself very briefly.

B: Brainstorm (*teacher's notes*) — 15 minutes
Get the each of students to brainstorm. Teacher's notes are available.

C: Discussion

1: Do you have a healthy balanced diet? — 10 minutes
Do you have a perfect diet? What is missing from your diet?
Do you eat any unhealthy food? Why is it unhealthy and what does it do to your body?

2: Food Safety (*teacher's notes*) — 10 minutes
Food safety is a huge issue now in China. Give examples of food which may be dangerous to eat. Why does China have this problem?

3: Which is the unhealthiest food? Why? — 10 minutes
Answer check by going around each student and writing their answers up on the white board. Now get them to vote for the worst one. Why is it the worst?

4: McDonald's and KFC (*teacher's notes*) — 10 minutes
Do you eat at McDonald's or KFC? How often? Think of five positive and five negative points about eating in these places.
This is a good opportunity to talk about intensive farming, growth hormones, antibiotics and battery farming.

Breaktime (5 minutes)

5: What is a vegetarian? What can a vegetarian eat? **5 minutes**
Ask the class and do this quickly, making a list on the white board for the Devil's Advocate later.
What is a vegan? If you only eat fish but not meat are you still a vegetarian?
"I'm a vegetarian but sometimes I eat a little bit of chicken." What is your opinion about this statement?

6: Think of five ways to lose weight **10 minutes**
Go on a diet, fasting, wire your teeth, liposuction, do lots of exercise.
The Atkins Diet is about the reduction of carbs in your food intake.

7: Memory Game **15 minutes**
Don't tell the students this is a memory game. Surprise them with it.
Write on the white board:
In pairs tell your classmate what you had for breakfast, lunch and dinner yesterday.
Did you enjoy it? What food do you love and hate?

After they have both finished get them to form new pairs and tell each other what their last partner said. Start and finish each student at the same time so the second person in each pair gets a turn.

D: Devil's Advocate

I want to be a vegetarian and I want you to join me. **10 minutes**

E: Role Play:

Over 60's Evening (*printables*) **15 minutes**

Part 1: (10 minutes)
Person A: You own a restaurant. You want to start an over 60's evening for the older people in your neighbourhood. Hire an expert chef to manage the evening.
Ask interview questions such as "What is your experience? Why are you interested in the job? How long have you been a chef?"
Person B: Expert Chef. Answer all questions. What special ideas do you have for over 60's evening?

Part 2: (5 minutes)
Person A: Owner. You had complaints from the customers. They didn't like the food. Some found it difficult and unsuitable to eat and one person choked on it.
Person B: Expert Chef. Make an excuse. It's not your fault.

F: Drilling the vocabulary and finish

Food
Additional Questions and Activities
These can be used in T18: Food, T19: Cooking and T20: Eating out

1: GM Food   10 minutes
What is GM food?
What are the advantages and disadvantages of GM food?

You can talk about tomato genes being crossed with those of deep sea fish to make them more resistant to cold.
You can also talk about the spider-goat that has been bred to produce Kevlar in its milk.

For good back up information on GM corporate signatures in plant DNA watch the film 'Food Inc'.

2: British English v American English   10 minutes
Think of three differences between British and American food vocabulary.
biscuit – cookie
sweets – candy
crisps – potato chips
chips – fries/ French fries
jam – jelly
aubergine – egg plant
courgette – zucchini

Answer Check

British eating times:
Lunch time is often called 'dinner time'.
An evening meal is often called 'tea time' and has nothing to do with drinking tea.
'Dinner' can used though is more formal.
'Supper' is normally a snack before bedtime.
American eating times:
An evening meal can be called 'dinner' or 'supper'.

3: Would you eat dog? Why or why not?   5 minutes
How about cat?

4: Is there any really expensive food you like?   5 minutes
What is it and how often do you have it?
When was the last time you had it? Where did you have it? Who was it with and what occasion was it? (past tense)

5: BTQ: What was the most expensive restaurant you ever went to?   10 minutes
Where was it? When did you go? Who with? What did you have? How was the food?
Why did you go there? Was it a special occasion? (past tense)

6: BTQ: What is the best food in China?   **10 minutes**
Why? Where is it from? How is it made? What's the worst? Why and where is it from?

7: BTQ: Have you ever been to a restaurant when the food was bad?   **10 minutes**
Where was it? Why was it so terrible? When did you go? Who with? How was the service? (past tense)

8: Steak   **5 minutes**
Teacher Talk Time:
Though ask the students what they know as you go along. Write it on the white board:
Blue, bloody, rare, medium rare, medium, medium well and well done. Well done is the hardest to do for any chef as it has to remain moist inside and not dry.
Ask the students how they like their steak?

Devil's Advocate

All men should be able to cook for their girlfriend or wife   **10 minutes**
You can only really do this one if you have the correct ratio of male and female students.

A vegetarian should not be able to eat fish   **10 minutes**

McDonalds is great place. Mmmm, it's delicious, healthy and nutritious.   **10 minutes**

Role Play:

Hire a new waiter/waitress   **15 minutes**

Part 1:   (10 minutes)
Person A: You own a restaurant (choose cuisine). Hire a new waitress/waiter.
Ask interview questions.
Why did you want to work in a restaurant? How do you take an order? What do you do if something is wrong?
Person B: Answer all the questions. Get the job!

Part 2:   (5 minutes)
Person A: Owner. You have had a lot of complains from the customers about your new waiter/waitress. Give them some advice and a warning.
Person B: Waiting Staff. Defend yourself. You are a professional.

Gluttonous member of staff   **5 minutes**
Person A: Boss. Your new member of staff is always eating in the office. Tell them that it must stop. You have already told them once before.
Person B: Employee. You work so hard you have to eat in the office.

Best Pizza **5 minutes**

Person A: Congratulations. Your shop has won an award for the best pizza in town. Talk about what different flavours you have on your menu.
Person B: CCTV interviewer. Continually ask follow up questions.

Pizza delivery driver **15 minutes**

Part 1: (10 minutes)

Person A: You ordered a pizza to be delivered to your apartment over two hours ago. You already phoned the shop, but it has still not arrived. Phone again and ask what has happened. Be angry.
Person B: You work in the restaurant. Answer the phone and make excuses why the pizza has still not been delivered.

Part 2: (5 minutes)

Person A: Finally after three hours the driver has arrived with your pizza. It is cold and you have already eaten now. Refuse to pay. Be angry.
Person B: Delivery driver. Make excuses as to why you are late. They must pay. Your boss will be angry if they don't.

Food
Printables

Over 60's Evening

Person A:

You own a restaurant.

You want to start an <u>over 60's</u> evening for the older people in your neighbourhood.

Hire an expert chef to manage the evening.

Ask interview questions such as
What is your experience?
Why are you interested in the job?
How long have you been a chef?
What ides to they have to make a great evening for the customers?

Person B: Expert Chef.

Answer all questions.

What special ideas do you have for <u>over 60's</u> evening?
Think about style and suitable food.
Think about atmosphere and music.
Think about anything special that the customers would like.

Food
Teacher's Notes

Vitamins:

Vitamin A is needed for your eyes.
  is found in oranges, ripe yellow fruits, leafy vegetables, carrots, pumpkin, squash, spinach and liver.

Vitamin B is needed for healthy skin and hair, is good for the immune system and red blood cells.
  is found in whole grains, potatoes, bananas, lentils, chilli peppers, beans yeast turkey, liver and tuna.
  There are eight types of Vitamin B often found in the same foods.

Vitamin C is needed to make collagen found in places like our joints. It's good for lowering the symptoms and prevention of colds and flu.
  is found in fruit and vegetables.

Vitamin D is required for strong bones.
  is absorbed from sunlight and found in fish, eggs, liver and mushrooms.

Vitamin E is needed for structural and functional maintenance of skeletal, cardiac, and muscles. It also assists in the formation of red blood cells. It is said, that it is good for night vision.
  is found in dark green leafy vegetables, vegetable oils, nuts, breakfast cereals, fruit juices and margarine.

Vitamin K helps your body by making protein for healthy bones and tissues.
  is found in leafy green vegetables such as spinach, also egg yolks and liver.

Food Safety in China

Your students will be able to talk about this all day. You might want to add another five minutes onto this discussion.

Here are examples of bad food safety that could end up under your nose.

- Fake mineral water: In Beijing at least half of it is fake
- Fake eggs: There are even special two week courses in making these as they are much cheaper than normal ones.
- Fake cooking oil: Also known as 'gutter oil' its discarded oil from restaurants.
- Fake organic: Anything labeled as 'organic' is likely not to be.
- Pesticides and wax: All fruit and vegetables have a super thick coating.
- Bad milk powder: The 2008 scandal was huge, though most people believe the problem still hasn't been entirely cleared up.
- Old shoes used in milk products and medicine capsule casings: Though there is no information to back up this claim, your students may well mention this anyway.

McDonald's and KFC

Being as objective as possible, there are clearly two sides this argument. Many studies and reports paint a highly negative picture of the harmful effects that this kind of food does to the body. However, many of your students will be blissfully unaware of these arguments that surround these fast food giants. Some will be visibly confused with their opinions limited to "It's convenient" and "It's delicious".

In terms of preparation for an IELTS or TOEFL exam, this is an essential discussion topic. It can be used in the following areas some of which are covered in Parts 2, 3 and the 'complete' version:

- T18: Food, T19: Cooking T20: Eating Out
- Hospitals, Basic Health Problems and First Aid, Health & Fitness
- Advertising
- The Environment and Natural Resources
- Animals and Pets

The films 'McLibel' and 'Supersize Me' are excellent resources.

Intensive Farming

Advantages

- The yield from intensive farming is high and helps feed our rapidly expanding population.
- Produce from intensive farming is much cheaper and therefore affordable for low income families.
- Production is possible with a smaller amount of land.

Disadvantages

- The livestock and poultry are injected with hormones and other chemicals to increase the yield. In terms of battery farming, a chicken can grow at an alarming rate reaching maturity in six weeks. A chicken may grow so fast and become so fat its legs wont work, forcing it to sit in piles of feces.
- The livestock and poultry are injected with antibiotics to keep them free from disease. Often the animals are kept in dirty conditions giving way to an increasing number of harmful diseases.
- Intensive farming involves the use of various kinds of chemical fertilizers, pesticides and insecticides.
- Intensive farming is also associated with farms that have overcrowded livestock in restricted and cramped areas. This leads to unsanitary conditions and various diseases.
- Forests are destroyed to create large open fields leading to soil erosion. This is particularly so regarding the soya production in the Amazon rainforest.
- Chemical fertilizers contaminate water sources such as lakes and rivers near the farming land.
- The fruit and vegetables grown from intensive farming are covered with invisible pesticide. These are hard to clean off and can be harmful to our health.

The film 'Food Inc' is an excellent resource for this topic.

Topic 19: Cooking

Additional questions for this topic can be found in T18: Food.

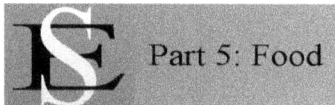

Part 5: Food   19

Cooking

Vocabulary and useful stuff

Ingredients: aubergine (UK), egg plant (US), salad
Cooking oil: sunflower, olive, soya, peanut oil and lard
Flavour ingredients: sugar, salt, vinegar, soy sauce, lemon juice, wine, beer, herbs, curry powder, red chillies, black pepper, garlic, ginger, butter, cheese
Utensils: Pots and pans, steamer, knife, fork, spoon, chopsticks ('kuaizi' in Chinese), spatula, chopping board, peeler
Process: wash, clean, chop, dice, slice, cut, fry, stir-fry, roast, bake, boil, steam, simmer, toast, grill
Recipe

Hello to new students   5 minutes

Where is your hometown? What do you do here? Are you a student or do you have a job? Why are you learning English? Which country do you want to go to? Introduce yourself very briefly.

Brainstorm: Ingredients (*see above*)   15 minutes

Ask the students what are the most important things when you are cooking?
Ingredients, utensils, process and recipe
Students will know a lot of vocabulary for fruit, vegetables and meat.
To one student, hold up all your fingers and ask them to tell you ten different vegetables.
To another, ten types of fruit.
To another, ten types of meat.
There will be a few things they may not know such as 'aubergine' (UK)/ 'eggplant'(US) and 'salad'.

Under ingredients write 'flavour' and get them to thing of as many different things we can use to bring flavour to our cooking. Go around each student one at a time and ask them individually. Write a list of everything. You will need this later in the class.

Discussion

1: Can you cook? If not, why not?   10 minutes
What is the best thing you can cook?
If you can't cook talk about your mother or father's best dish.

Brainstorm: Utensils (*see above*)   **10 minutes**
Get the students to think of one utensil we use in the kitchen.
Write a list down the board next to the ingredients.

Discussion

2: Romantic candle lit dinner for two.   **10 minutes**
If you were going to cook a romantic candle lit dinner for two, what would it be? What special flavours would you use and why? What would you have for dessert?
Answer Check

Brainstorm: Process (*see above*)   **10 minutes**
Get the students to think of one simple verb we can use when cooking.
Write a list down the board next to the utensils.

You could also ask, what is the difference between steaming and boiling?

Breaktime (5 minutes)

Discussion: Recipes

3: How do you prepare an onion?   **10 minutes**
Students should use sequencing such as 'First, second, next and last'.
Use the vocabulary on the white board for utensils and process.
Answer check.

4: How do you make a delicious chicken and salad sandwich?   **15 minutes**
Students should use sequencing such as 'First, second, next and last'.
Give them a few more new words before you start and drill it with them: *slice of bread, loaf of bread, two loaves of bread, margarine and spread (v)*.
Make sure they understand that it should be a delicious sandwich. They should use the flavour list on the white board.
Answer Check: Ask some of your students to explain their recipes.

Devil's Advocate

Microwave cooking is not real cooking.   **10 minutes**

Cooking is an essential skill that should be taught in middle school.   **10 minutes**

Role Play

Celebrity Chef (*printables*)   **10 minutes**

If you can, put students into threes, though pairs is also ok.

Person A: You are a famous celebrity chef in China. Everyone has heard about your cooking. You have written your own cook books and have your own TV show.
Even Xi Jinping and his wife Peng Liyuan love your cooking and often ask you to cook for them.
Talk about why your food is so popular on CCTV.
What are some of your special recipes and what special flavours do you use?
Person B/C: CCTV interviewer(s). This is very exciting. Continually ask follow up questions. Where do they get their ingredients from? Where did they get their recipes from? Why did they want to be a chef. Are there any other famous people they cook for? What is Xi Jinping and Peng Liyuan's favourite dish? Why?

Drilling the vocabulary and finish

Cooking
Teacher's Notes

Most of your students won't have much of an idea about how to cook. Even if they are in their mid twenties their parents may still be cooking for them. Their parents say that learning to cook detracts from more important matters like studying.

Many people who live in big cities may eat in a restaurant twice a day and buy street food for breakfast. They may also have limited or no access to a kitchen if they are sharing an apartment or dormitory. Some landlords rent out a space in their apartment and fill it with as many people as they can such as wages are generally so low and renting is expensive.

Additional Questions & Activities
Go to Topic 18: Food for anything extra. Everything there can also be used for this topic and T20: Eating Out.

Cooking
Printables

Celebrity Chef:

Person A: You are a famous celebrity chef in China

Everyone has heard about your cooking.
You have written your own cook books and have your own TV show.

Even Xi Jinping and his wife Peng Liyuan love your cooking and often ask you to cook for them.

Talk about why your food is so popular on CCTV.

What are some of your special recipes and what special flavours do you use?

Persons B &C: CCTV interviewers

This is very exciting.

Continually ask follow up questions:
Where do they get their ingredients from?
Which flavours do they use?
Where did they get their recipes from?
Why did they want to be a chef?
Are there any other famous people they cook for? Which dishes are their favourites?
What is Xi Jinping and Peng Liyuan's favourite dish? Why?

Topic 20: Eating Out

Additional questions for this topic can be found in T18: Food

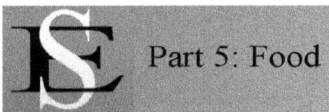 Part 5: Food

Eating Out

Vocabulary and useful stuff

Cuisine
Italian: spaghetti, salami, mozzarella
Service
Mug, white/black tea or coffee
Delicacy
Etiquette, table manners
Slurping, chomping
Four course meal, (appetizer/starter, salad, entrée, dessert)
Chef's special

A: Hello to new students — 5 minutes
Where is your hometown? What do you do here? Are you a student or do you have a job? Why are you learning English? Which country do you want to go to? Introduce yourself very briefly.

B: Brainstorm — 10 minutes
Get the students to quickly brainstorm on the topic. Write down anything useful they may say.

C: Discussion

1: International Cuisine — 10 minutes
If you could choose any restaurant from around the world to eat in tonight which one would it be and why? Students are not allowed to choose Chinese food.
Think of six key words for it for, example, Japanese cuisine: *Sushi, miso soup, okayu (porridge), wasabi (horse radish), whale and dolphin.*

2: Service — 10 minutes
Give three or four examples of good and bad service in a restaurant.
Answer Check

3: Recommend a great restaurant — 10 minutes
What kind of food is it? Where is it? What is the service like? When did you last go?

4: How do you like your tea/coffee? — 10 minutes
Teacher Talk Time:

In England tea is the most common drink. In America it's coffee.
It's very important to make it correctly for people, especially for your boss, clients or if you have guests.
You should ask "How do you take it?" or "How do you like it?"
This means white or black? Sugar or no sugar? How many sugars? People use sugar cubes or a tea spoon to measure.
Teacher: Ask each student "Tea or coffee?" and "How do you take it?"
Student: Answer quickly with "Coffee, black no sugar" or "Tea, white one sugar".

Breaktime (5 minutes)

5: Delicacy   10 minutes
Think of one or two delicacies from around the world, for example, caviar, Koreans and Chinese people in the far north like eating dog, in France people like frog's legs and snails.
Is there any food you would not eat?

6: Four course meal   5 minutes
Write the heading on the white board. Ask the students what they know as you go through it, giving examples of each one.
1: Starter/ appetiser
2: Salad
3: Main course/entrée
4: Dessert

7: Etiquette   10 minutes
Think of examples of good and bad table manners.
In the West we really dislike anyone making a noise when they are eating. Also eating with your mouth open is a big no no. Cover your mouth if you want to talk and eat at the same time. Don't spit out food; use a tissue or napkin.

D: Devil's Advocate

McDonalds and KFC are not 'real' restaurants.   **10 minutes**

E: Role Play:

Order food in a restaurant (*printables*)   **25 minutes**
An extra five minutes has been added into this lesson plan so you have time to explain things to the students and give the activity some breathing space.

Go to Printables 1 for the Wonderful Food Menu. Give students 2-3 minutes to look at it. Use also, the flash cards for terrible food.

Put your students into small groups of three or four. Make one the waiter or waitress. They don't have to stand up when they do this.

Part 1: (5 minutes)

Person A: Waiter or waitress. Welcome your customers. Use Sir or Madame and be as polite as possible. Recommend the Chef's Special. Take their order
Persons B, C & D: Customers. Order drinks and an entrée.

Part 2: (5 minutes)

Customers use the Wonderful Food Menu (*printables 1*)
Persons B, C & D: Customers. That food was wonderful. Give lots of praise to the waiter. Be really enthusiastic.
Person A: Waiter or waitress. Greatly accept the praise and tell them why the food is so good.

Part 3: (10 minutes)

Customers use the flash cards drawn from a bag (*printables 2*)
Persons B, C & D: Customers. That food was terrible. Tell the waiter/waitress why. Refuse to pay the bill.
Person A: Waiter or waitress. It's not your fault. Make excuses. They must pay!

F: Drilling the vocabulary and finish

Eating Out
Printables 1

Wonderful Food Menu

Delicious

A joy   there was so much

The dessert was mouth watering

Heavenly   **Yummy**

Extremely flavourful

Wonderful service – So friendly

                       I couldn't stop eating

My compliments to the chef

The starter was so fresh

                 The meat melted in your mouth

Really great   juicy

        I'll definitely be coming back again

I would like to leave a huge tip

I just love it here so much

                 I will tell ALL of my friends

Perfect   Really special

Printables 2

Flash Cards:

The waiter/waitress put their finger in my food	**The food is cold**
The food tastes like it was microwaved and it has a strange smell	**Too sweet**
There was a fingernail in it	**Too spicy**
Raw meat	**Too salty**

There is a long hair in my food	The portion is too small
Burnt	Wrong food
Too oily	Dirty plate & cutlery
Unfriendly Service	Undercooked
An insect in my food	The vegetables are old

Appendix A

Grammar at a Glance

For those who may not be one hundred percent clued up on grammar, here is a list of the basics with examples. If a student asks you something you aren't sure about, the guide will quickly help you solve the problem. They aren't in alphabetical order so if you want to find anything just hit search.

Article:
Definite Article: *the* is used to restrict the meaning of a noun and give us information about it **Indefinite Article:** a determiner that expresses non specific reference, such as *a, an,* or *some*

Preposition: used before nouns, pronouns, or other substantives to form phrases functioning as modifiers of verbs, nouns, or adjectives, and that typically express a spatial, temporal, or other relationship, **as in, on, by, to, since, at, of, off, with.**

A part of speech that indicates the relationship, often spatial, of one word to another, for example, 'She paused at the door', 'This apple is ripe for picking'; and 'They talked the matter over face to face.' Some common prepositions are ***at, by, for, from, in, into, on, to,* and *with.***

Noun: Nouns are a class of words that are subjects of verbs and prepositions. They can be used in plurals. Nouns often refer to people, places, things, states and quantities.

Subject Pronoun: What are you looking at? e.g. **I, me, you, him,** he, she, this, **who, what** takes the place of a noun.

Verb: Verbs are used to describe actions, states and relationships between two or more things.

Adjective: Adjectives describe and modify nouns or pronouns. They can be before such as the red car or after such as the car is red.

Adverb: Adverbs are used to modify a **verb, an adjective, or another adverb**:
        1: Mary sings *terribly*
        2: David is *extremely* stupid
        3: This car goes *incredibly* slow

In 1, the adverb *beautifully* tells us how Mary sings. In 2, *extremely* tells us the degree to which David is stupid. Finally, in 3, the adverb *incredibly* tells us how slowly the car goes.

Many adverbs end in ly e.g. slowly, quickly, softly, suddenly, and gradually
        Adjectives: slow, quick, soft, sudden, gradual

Adverbs are gradable e.g. soft = very softly, extremely quickly, really gently
These modifying words are also adverbs and called **Degree Adverbs**
(almost, barely, entirely, highly, quite, slightly, totally, and utterly)

Comparative Adverbs: use more e.g. more recently, more frequently
Superlative Adverbs: use most e.g. most recently, most frequently

Adverbs do not modify nouns.

Phrasal Verbs: When a verb is added to a preposition or adverb the meaning of the verb changes, for example, 'My car broke down last night' > break down. Phrasal verbs can have more than one meaning. In this case someone who is upset can break down.
There are around 3,000 phrasal verbs. They are impossible to quantify due to informal and formal usage.

Some are <u>separable</u> and can be split up and still form a sentence:
'Take off your coat' > 'Take your coat off.'
'She looked up the word' > 'She looked the word up'
'He ate up all his dinner' >'He ate all his dinner up'.

Some are <u>inseparable</u>
'We are looking into the problem.' (would be *looking the problem into*)
'Look after the children.' (would be *look the children after*)
'I called on a friend' (would be I called a friend on)

Predicate: Every complete sentence contains two parts: a **subject** and a **predicate**. The subject is what (or whom) the sentence is about, while the predicate tells something about the subject. In the following sentences, the predicate is placed in brackets ( ), while the subject is highlighted.

Barry (runs).

Barry and his dog (run on the hill every morning).

Coordinating Conjunction:
join or link words or phrases together within a sentence. Some coordinating conjunctions are **and, yet, for, and but.**

Subordinating Conjunctions:
are found at the beginning of independent clauses. Some common subordinating conjunctions are **if, although, since and while.**

Demonstrative Determiner:
used to demonstrate the identity of the thing referenced by the following noun; in English, they include **this, these, that and those** e.g. 'I like this dictionary' the word 'this' is a demonstrative determiner.

Clause:
is a group of words which act as a single unit and is built round a verb, for example, 'he lives in the UK'

Compound and complex sentences contain two or more clauses:

Simple: **'Barry is living in the UK'.**

Compound: **'He lives in the UK, but his family is still in China'.**

Complex: 'While his family is still in China, Barry is staying with friends'.

Relative Clauses:
A sentence or statement that can give extra information. They can bring two parts of a sentence together to make dialogue more fluent.
To do this we use **relative pronouns,** for example, 'A girl is talking to Tom. Do you know the girl?'>'Do you know the girl who is talking to Tom?'

- **That:** Subject or Object pronoun for people, animals or things
- **Who:** Subject or Object for people
- **Which:** Subject or Object for animals or things
- **Which:** Referring to a whole sentence, for example, 'He couldn't say the letter T which surprised me'.
- **Whose:** Possession for animals or things

If Clauses:
There are three types of conditional if-clauses
- Conditional Sentence 1: Here it is possible and also very probable that the condition will be completed:

Form: If + simple present = will (future)
E.g.: If I see his wife, Ill tell her he's down the bar.

- Conditional Sentence 2: Here it is possible but unlikely, that the condition will be completed.

Form: If + simple past = conditional (would + infinitive)
E.g.: If I saw his wife, I would tell her he was down the bar.

- Conditional Sentence 3: Here it is impossible that the condition will be completed because it is referring to the past.

Form: If + past perfect = conditional (would have + past participle)
Example: If I had seen his wife, I would have told her he was down the bar.

3rd Person – Simple present tense: he, she, them and they

'Joe walks down the street with his hands in his pockets'.
'She stares into the mirror at the failure before her'.
- **He/She**: Third person singular
- **It**: Third person singular
- **They**: Third person plural

2nd Person – Simple present tense: You stare into the mirror at the failure before you.
- **You**: Second person singular

1st Person – Simple present tense: I stare into the mirror at the failure before me 1st
- **I**: First person singular
- **We**: First person plural

VERB FORMS

Lexical Verb: contain some sort of meaning and can stand alone, e.g. 'I love chocolate'

Auxiliary Verb: 1: help the lexical verb e.g. 'He's watching TV' = 'is'
        2: to make the sentence 'He lives here' negative, add does to make 'He doesn't live here'
        3: to create a question 'Does he live here?'

Remember: **be, do and have** can function in different forms.
Remember: be has different present and past forms: am, are is, has and were
However, all three can be used as lexical and auxiliary verbs aswell e.g.
'I didn't arrive on time' + auxiliary
'I did my homework' = lexical only

Modal Auxiliary Verbs: carry meaning: can, could, may, might, will, would, shall, should, must, need, ought to and dare e.g. 'I must go'.

Base Form of a verb: e.g. 'He listens' the base form is to listen.

Present Participle ends in 'ing'. Are verb forms used to function as an adjective. They are the only verb forms that stay completely regular (see below).

The present participle is used with an auxiliary to express the progressive aspect (see below)
'That film is very exciting'

Past Participle ends in 'ed' or 'en' and it has two functions:

1) Adjective

E.g.: This car **is** heated. (Verb: 'is'; Adjective 'heated')
E.g.: We had **a** heated discussion. (Adjective 'heated')
E.g.: I had seen it, I have seen it, I will have seen it, It was seen

As an adjective, the past participle occurs after the verb **BE** (is, am, was, were, been) or it modifies a noun.

2) As part of a verb

E.g.: The stove **has** heated the room. (Verb: 'has'; Part of a verb: 'heated')

As a part of a verb, the past participle occurs with the verb **HAVE** (have, has, had).

Gerunds: verb + ing 'I'm working as hard as I can' or 'Running is good for your health'
They are only formed with the infinitive + ing
Note the difference between a progressive which uses is was has have would etc
Gerund: A verb form with 'ing' forming a noun, for example, 'I am going running'.

S-Forms: she plays, he works

Ing-Forms: playing, running

Finite Verbs: form the main part of a sentence. Non-finite is therefore an infinitive, gerund or participle

Infinitives: Verbs that have to before them. Sometimes they will be no to but the verb still remains the infinitive such as feel, hear, help, make, let, see and watch.

Action Verbs/State Verbs: 'Nigel went to school' = action. 'I'm buying a new car' = action
                'Nigel was busy' = state. 'I need a new car' = state
'Action' is something happening e.g. do, go buy, play stop, take
'State' is something staying the same e.g. be, doubt, believe, know, want, need, seem

Regulars Verbs: Most verbs are regular. If we add 'ed' to them to put them into the past, the spelling or pronunciation is the same. 'I walked' can be used in past tense or past participle,
'I walked', 'I have walked'

Irregular Verbs: (around 400) Their sound or spelling change when we put them into the past, for example, 'make = made', 'give = gave(s) or given (pp)', 'saw = seen'
Was, bite, bring, break, bought, and began
Some irregular verbs are the same in past simple and past participle e.g. make/made/made

Mixing different verb forms to create phrases:
1. e.g. Combine irregular v 'have' as an auxiliary to the – **ing** lexical 'be'
'I have been'
2. e.g. Combine modal 'should' with base form 'have' and past participle of 'study'
'I should have studied'

Past Tense refers to a verb, (remember that past participles are not verbs.)

E.g.: The stove heated the room.
E.g.: I saw it

In the example above, the word heated doesnt do the following things:

It doesn't occur with BE (is, am, was, were, been)
It doesn't occur with HAVE (have, has, have)
It doesnt modify a noun (argument)

'heated' functions all by itself. It's a verb, and the 'ed' ending tells us it's a past tense verb

Present Perfect: Actually still refers to a past event: We use the Present Perfect to say that an action happened at an unspecified time before now. The exact time is not important. You CANNOT use the Present Perfect with specific time expressions such as: yesterday, one year ago, last week, when I was a child, when I lived in China, at that moment, that day, one day, etc. We CAN use the Present Perfect with unspecific expressions such as: ever, never, once, many times, several times, before, so far, already, yet, etc.
Present Perfect examples:
I **have seen** that film twenty times.
I think I **have met** him once before.
There **have been** many earthquakes in Japan.
People **have travelled** to the Moon.
People **have not travelled** to Jupiter.
Have you **read** the book yet?

Nobody **has** ever **climbed** that mountain.
A: **Has** there ever **been** a war in Europe?
B: Yes, there **has been** a war in the Europe.

Past Perfect:
The Past Perfect expresses the idea that something occurred before another action in the past. It can also show that something happened before a specific time in the past.
I **had** never **seen** such a beautiful beach before I went to Kauai.
I did not have any money because I **had lost** my wallet.
Tony knew Istanbul so well because he **had visited** the city several times.

Future perfect:
The Future Perfect expresses the idea that something will occur before another action in the future. It can also show that something will happen before a specific time in the future.
By next November, I **will have received** my promotion.
By the time he *gets* home, she **is going to have cleaned** the entire house.
I **am not going to have finished** this test by 3 o'clock.

Progressive Aspect: also called Continuous uses 'to be'

A. Present progressive = am + (base form + -ing): I am working OR is + (base form + -ing):
She is eating. OR are + (base form + -ing): We are studying.

1. A planned activity: Sofia is starting school at CEC tomorrow

2. An activity that is occurring right now: Jan is watching TV right now.

3. An activity that is in progress, although not actually occurring at the time of speaking: Sara is learning English at CEC.

B. Past progressive = was + (base form + -ing): I was working. OR were + (base form + -ing): They were eating.

1. A past activity in progress while another activity occurred: At 6:00 yesterday I was eating dinner. The phone rang while I was eating.

2. Two past activities in progress at the same time: While I was answering the phone, my wife was cooking dinner.

C. Future progressive = will be + (base form + -ing): I will be working. He will be eating.

An activity that will be in progress: This time next year we will be living in Canada.

We can also ask about someone's plans using the future progressive.
Will you be going to Canada next year?

D. Present perfect progressive = have + (base form + -ing): I have been working. OR has + (base form + -ing): She has been eating.

1. This tense emphasizes the duration of an activity that began in the past and continues into the present. It often uses time words or phrases. It may be used to refer to continuing activity that is recent: He has been painting houses all summer. I've been studying English for 2 years.

2. It may be used to refer to continuing activity that is recent: He has been going to school at CEC.

E. Past perfect progressive = had + (base form + -ing): I had been working. He had been eating.

When the teacher arrived, I had been waiting almost 10 minutes. He was out of breath because he had been running to catch the bus.

F. Future perfect progressive = will have + (base form + -ing): I will have been working. She will have been eating. This tense emphasizes the duration of a continuing activity in the future that ends before another activity or time in the future.

By 2003 Janet will have been studying English at CEC for 3 years. By 9:45 tonight I will have been sitting in class for 2 hours and 45 minutes.

Active Verbs (voice):
In active sentences, the thing doing the action is the subject of the sentence and the thing receiving the action is the object. Most sentences we say are active.

(Thing doing action) + (verb) + (thing receiving action)

The teacher (subject) teaches (active verb) the students (object)
Students (subject) do (active verb) their homework (object)

Passive Verbs (voice):
In passive sentences, the thing receiving the action is the subject of the sentence and the thing doing the action is optionally included near the end of the sentence.

(Thing receiving action) + (be) + (past participle of verb) + (by) + (thing doing action)

The students (sub) are taught (passive verb) by the teacher (object)
Homework (sub) is done (passive verb) by the students (object)

Appendix B

Using Phonetics

A basic knowledge of phonetics is very useful as most Chinese students use it as a guide in their pronunciation. Write the relevant symbol under vocabulary if they are having problems with it. The various symbols plus examples are below. The sounds where students have the most frequent difficulties are interlined.

iː fleece	ɪ minute	ʊ foot	uː group	ɪə near	eɪ face	
e head	ə common	ɜː nurse	ɔː thought	ʊə store	ɔɪ choice	əʊ show
æ track	ʌ love	ɑː start	ɒ lot	eə fair	aɪ high	aʊ round
p plant	b black	t trust	d ladder	tʃ church	dʒ judge	k key	g get
f future	v heavy	θ thank	ð this	s soon	z zoo	ʃ ship	ʒ usual
m mountain	n Nigeria	ŋ king	h heavy	l valley	r robin	w windy	j useful

Consonants	**Vowels**
p: pen, copy, happen	ɪ: kit, bid, hymn, minute
b: back, baby, job	e: dress, bed, head, many
t: tea, tight, button	æ: trap, bad
d: day, ladder, odd	ɒ: lot, odd, wash
k: key, clock, school	ʌ: strut, mud, love, blood
g: get, giggle, ghost	ʊ: foot, good, put
tʃ: church, match, nature	iː: fleece, sea, machine
dʒ: judge, age, soldier	eɪ: face, day, break
f: fat, coffee, rough, photo	aɪ: price, high, try
v: view, heavy, move	ɔɪ: choice, boy
θ: thing, author, path	uː: goose, two, blue, group
ð: this, other, smooth	əʊ: goat, show, no
s: soon, cease, sister	aʊ: mouth, now, brown
z: zero, music, roses, buzz	ɪə: near, here, weary
ʃ: ship, sure, national	eə: square, fair, various
ʒ: pleasure, vision	ɑː: start, father
h: hot, whole, ahead	ɔː: thought, law, north, war
m: more, hammer, sum	ʊə: poor, jury, cure
n: nice, know, funny, sun	ɜː: nurse, stir, learn, refer
ŋ: ring, anger, thanks, sung	ə: about, common, standard
l: light, valley, feel	i: happy, radiate, glorious
r: right, wrong, sorry, arrange	u: thank you, influence, situation
j: use, beauty, few	
w: wet, one, when, queen	
ʔ: (glottal stop) department, football (often used in the UK)	

Appendix C

Common Student Errors

I frequently get worried looking students coming up to me asking me how they can improve their English before their exam. Many are taking it for the second or third time having not attained the score they need to go overseas. Actually most problems are very common, straightforward and identifiable almost immediately. The real issue is that their errors are habitual, having been ingrained since middle school and thus making them really difficult to iron out.

Recently one of my students was scratching her head wondering what she did wrong in her IELTS; after three attempts the highest she'd got was a 5.5 when she really needed at least a 6. She'd been working really hard and clearly things had gotten the better of her. Blowing he nose into a tissue I asked if she was ok

"I catch cold" was her painful reply!

Here is a list of some of the most common mistakes made in class.
- Basic pronunciation errors.
- Some can be referred as 'Chinglish' which means the direct translation from Chinese into English.
- Some things are straight out of a textbook and may have little to do with the real world.
- General poor use of simple grammar. You don't have to be a grammar wiz when it comes to student correction. After a while you will notice that you are correcting the same errors again and again.

Pronunciation

Refer to Appendix B: Using Phonetics.
Phonetics are in British English.

Lo**ve**/**Bl**oo**d**/**M**u**d** – Phonetics: /ləv/bləd/məd/
Error: /læv/blæd/mæd/
The /ə/ sound is replaced with a pronounced /æ/ saying 'LAV' or 'BLAD'.

Rou**nd**/**Br**ow**n**/**Fr**ow**n** – Phonetics: /raʊnd/ braʊn/fraʊn
Error: /rɑnd/brɑn/frɑn/
The /aʊ/ is replaced by /ɑ/ sounding like 'RAAND' or "BRAAN'.

Wi**ll**/**M**i**ll**/**Sk**i**ll** – Phonetics: / wɪl / mɪl / skɪl /
Error: / w i ː l / m i ː l / sk i ː l /
The /ɪ/ is replaced by / i ː / changing the meaning of the word to 'WHEAL, MEAL'.

Us**ual**/**C**a**sual**/**G**en**re** – Phonetics: / ju ː ʒəwəl/ kæʒwəl/ ʒɑnrə
Many students will be able to make the /ʒ/ sound when you ask them, but in normal conversation they will forget it instantly.
Error: /ju ː ju ː ɔr/ kæ ju ː ɔr/jɑnrə/
The individual may say 'U YOU AL/, CA YOU AL or YANRE'
Many also have difficulty making the last 'L' sound, instead substituting it with an 'AW' sound, for example, 'U YOU AW' and 'CA YOU AW'.

This/**Th**at/O**th**er – Phonetics: / ðɪs / ðæt / əðər
Error: /zɪs / zæt / əzər/
The /ð/ is replaced by /z/ creating 'ZIS, ZAT' or 'OZZER'

Thanks/Au**th**or/Mou**th** – Phonetics: / θæŋks / ɔ ː θə / maʊθ/
Error: / sæŋks / ɔ ː sə / pɑ ː s /
The /θ/ is replaced by /s/ forming 'SANKS', 'AUSOR' or 'MOUSE'

Violin/**V**ery/Ha**v**e – Phonetics: / vaɪəlɪn / veri ː / hæv /
Error: /waɪəlɪn / weri ː / hæw /
The /v/ is replaced by /w/ forming 'WIOLIN', 'WERY' or 'HOW'

Quality/**Qu**antity/**Qu**alify – Phonetics: /kwɒləti ː / kwɒntəti ː / kwɒləfɪ
Error: /kɒləti ː / kɒntəti ː / kɒləfaɪ/ Note the /w/ is omitted forming 'KAALITY'.
Also there is not normally any difficulty with 'qui' words such as 'quick' and 'quiet'.

Tragedy/Trick/Tree – Phonetics: / **trædʒədi / trɪk / triː** /
Error: / twædʒədi / twɪk / twiː /
The /r/ is replaced by /w/ thus forming 'TWAGEDY' or 'TWICK'.

Towel/Vehicle/ Critical – Phonetics: / **taʊəl / viːɪkəl / krɪtɪkəl /**
Error: / taʊ ɔː / viː ɪkɔː / krɪtɪk ɔː / Here the learner is unable to make the /l / sound ending the word, instead replacing it with / ɔː / forming 'TOWAW' or 'VEHICAW'.

Little/Bottle/Title – Phonetics: / **lɪtəl / bɒtəl / taɪtəl /**
This is an interesting pronunciation error. In the US, if there is a double or single 't' after a vowel it is often changed to a 'd' sound. In both British and American English the /ə/ is omitted with the 't/d' and 'l' being made at the same time, for example.
/ lɪtl / bɒtl / taɪtl /
This allows us to focus on making the 'l' clear and pronounced.
Error: / lɪtɔː / bɒtɔː / taɪtɔː /
As above, the /l/ is replaced with / ɔː / forming 'LITTAW' or 'BOTTAW'. The same applies to words with a 'd' after a vowel such as 'medal' or 'idle'.

The addition of an unnecessary schwa sound / ə /
Orange/Finish/ Few
Error: / ɒrɪndʒ ə / fɪnɪʃ ə / fjuː ə /
This normally happens after the student has said something that sounds like it ends in a consonant forming 'ORANGE ER', 'FINISH ER' or 'FEW ER'.

In addition to this, a schwa may be placed in between two consonants, for example, Adverb/Football/Hardback
Error: / æd ə vɜːb / fʊt ə bɔːl / hɑː d ə bæk /
Sounds like 'ADUVERB', 'FOOTUBALL' or HARDUBACK'.

These common problems that are incredibly deep rooted. They are only ironed out by continually reminding the student at key stages of each lesson such as the beginning, after break and at the end of the lesson (so not to interfere with their fluency). Students must really understand and identify this problem and be committed to changing the way that they speak.

Chinglish

How do you or can you say (something)?
Error: How to say? / How to spell? This comes from the direct translation of Chinese to English: 'zen me shuo?' / 'zen me pin xie'.
This is the most common mistake made by Chinese students. It is an ingrained habit that you will hear everywhere.

What does it/this mean?
Error: What is meaning? / What's meaning? This comes from the direct translation of 'shenme yisi?' or 'what meaning?'

It's been a while / It's been a long time used if we haven't seen someone for a while.
Error: Although everyone knows '**Long time no see**' we rarely use it. Chinese students may often use this as it is common to say 'Hao jiu bu jian' which is its direct translation.

I like to use the computer/ play computer games
Error: 'I like to play computer' is less of a problem from direct translation, rather than one of laziness that generalises both statements. Firstly it is missing the preposition 'with' and also the possessive pronoun 'my'. Normally we would say 'use my computer' and 'play (computer) games'.

I really like it
Error: 'I very like it'. This unfortunate sentence comes from the translation of 'feichang xihuan' (very like). Unfortunately the Chinese language has no way of modifying a verb as in English which places 'very much' after the verb. In colloquial English we can say 'really like' instead of 'very' before the verb. 'Very enjoy' is another example of this.

Another problem that can occur along side the misuse of 'very' is the confusion between 'like' and 'enjoy'. Because of this you may hear '**I am very liking it**'. The word 'like' expresses a state or condition so it is not used as a continuous verb. If used to give approval of something it can be used in the continuous sense though this is rare.

I have a lot of money
Error: 'I have much money'. This common error originates from the use of 'hen duo' which covers, 'much, many' and 'a lot of'. Most students will be aware that 'a lot of' can be used with both countable and uncountable and that 'many' can be used with countable nouns. However though this is possible, it is not common to use either 'many' or 'much' in positive sentences. Normally we use them with 'do not', for example, 'I don't have much money' or 'There isn't much time to eat dinner'.

Text Book English

Nice to meet you.
Error: This should be used only on the first time of meeting. However, it is often mistakenly used instead of 'Nice to see you (again)'.
'Nice to meet you' is also used formally and may be replaced with something more colloquial.

Q: How are you? A: Fine!
Technically there is no error here but in reality native English speakers rarely ask this question. Though this will vary from country to country we would normally say something far more informal. When we give an answer it is also common to say 'thanks' after our answer followed by 'How about you?'

Basic Grammar

Present v past tense
The most common error you will hear is your students keeping everything in the present tense. Though your students will be aware of its importance, unless you remind them they will naturally keep speaking in the present where it is necessary to be speaking in the past or future. Think of as many activities as you can to keep them focused on it.

Why did you buy this?
Error: 'Why you buy this? / Why you like it?' is missing the auxiliary verb 'do', for example, 'Why did you buy this?' or 'Why do you like it?'

He/She
Because 'ta' is used in Chinese for both male and female (him/her and 'ta de' meaning his or hers), they are frequently misused, for example, 'he is going to have a baby soon' or 'she is going to get married to Susan.'
To Western ears it may sound laughable, but it is a big problem for some learners and another difficult habit to iron out.

Give him/her
Error: 'give he/she'. Here the objective 'him/her' is mistakenly replaced by the pronoun 'he/she'. The object 'him/her' is meant to work with a verb, in this case 'give'.

Give them
Error: 'give he or she' / 'give him or her'. In this case 'them' can be used for anyone without reference to sex. Students may be think that 'them' only refers to the plural and so develop this long winded way of saying things, for example, 'When I have a child, I want him or her to be happy'.

Have and Has
Though they are very important when describing possession or when using the perfect tense, 'have' and 'has' are frequently confused. There are only really a few basic rules to this and they are definitely worth remembering.

For Possession
He has a new car/ I have a new car. Error: 'He have a new car'.
'Have': Used with the pronouns 'I' and 'you' and plural nouns.
1: 'I have a class today' or 'You have a student waiting for you'.
2: 'Students have a lot of pressure', 'We have a class' or 'They have a class'
'Has': Used with the third person singular: 'he, she, it'.
'She has a new student to teach', 'It has a written exam'.

'Have got' and 'has got' have the same meaning, for example, 'I have got no class today' means the same as 'I have no class today'. 'He has got a new student to teach' is the same as 'He has a new student to teach'.

Verb Tenses
Present Perfect
'Have': 'I have been to class a few times', 'You have to read that book one day'.
'Has':   'He had to go to class a few times' or 'It has to be sometime in the near future'.
Past Perfect
'Have': I had to go to class before I start the next semester', 'He had already completed the exam before the class ended' or 'They had gone to the UK before passing their test'.

'Have to' as a modal verb: subject + modal verb (have to/has to/had to) + verb
'I/you/students/we/they have to go to class, 'He/she/it has to get there on Friday',
'I/you/we/they/he/she/it had to'

In four day's time / Four days later
Error: 'In four days later' where past and future become confused. Normally someone is trying to refer to something happening n the past. 'In four days (time)' is a prediction normally attached with 'will be going to' whereas 'later' is a simple way to say afterwards.

Let's go and have dinner/ I want to eat seafood tonight
Error: 'Let's go and have a dinner' or **'I want to eat the seafood tonight'** It is very common for articles 'a, an' and 'the' to be used with uncountable nouns especially when an adjective is preceding it, for example, 'I have a casual clothes'.

You will also hear 'the England' or 'the France'. Most of the time there is no article before a country name unless the name indicates more than one area is covered or it is a republic, for example, The UK, The USA, The PRC, The USSR, The Czech Republic or The Republic of Ireland. Great Britain is excluded from this list though we can say The British Isles.

This is exciting/ I am excited
Error: 'This is excited / I am exciting'. 'Exciting' is an adjective that describes someone's emotion <u>about</u> something. 'Excited' is an adjective <u>informing</u> you that something has influenced your emotions. Other examples that are commonly used are 'boring/bored', 'surprising/surprised' or 'interesting/interested'.

Further problems occur when a present participle (+ing) or past participle (+ 'ed') are used incorrectly. Always use present participles when the noun you are referring to <u>creates</u> the action. If the noun receives the action, use past participles, for example, "The class is interesting" and 'I was interested'.
One single problem that frequently occurs is between the uncountable noun 'health' and adjective 'healthy'.
Error: 'That is bad for your healthy' or **'He is very health'.**

There is not enough time
Error: 'There is <u>no</u> enough time' is another common error. 'No' is never used before 'any, much, many' or 'enough'. It can be used in before other adjectives that accompany a noun, for example, 'no fast cars'.

He doesn't have enough time
Error: 'He don't have enough time' should be 'doesn't'.
'I, you, we' and 'they' go with 'don't'.
'He, she' and 'it' goes with 'doesn't'.

Do you have a hobby?
Error: 'Do you have some hobby?' Mistakes involving plurals and singulars are very common. Here it should be either, 'a hobby' or 'some hobbies'. Often the learner is thinking separately and making an incorrect connection between the adjective and noun rather than seeing them together as a single form. Other common errors are: 'There is some', 'There have some', 'The advantages is', 'The book are' and so on.

I need to go shopping
Error: 'I need to go <u>to</u> shopping'. You can't put a preposition before a gerund. This is a mistake where the learner is trying to do too much and is a sign of uncertainty. Can say 'I need to go to the shops' (prep + definite article + noun)

She work<u>s</u> very hard
Error: 'She work very hard'. The simple present tense is one of the most common. Regarding the third person (he, she, it) you must add an 's'. Other errors could be 'He go to work', 'He cook for me' or 'She go by bus'.

I'm mak<u>ing</u> a plan
Error: 'I'm make a plan'. Misuse of the present progressive <u>am</u> + <u>base form</u> + <u>ing</u>
Other examples could be 'She is cook (ing) a meal' or 'I am go (ing) to my office.

Appendix D

Quick Fire Activities

During class there are other things you can do to sprinkle in with your existing lesson plans. Use these especially if you have been teaching the same topic and are looking to add something new.

If you need to inject some more energy into class then also use some of these activities. I use them all the time just to keep things varied, mainly around discussion times.

Forms of Connected Speech

This essential aspect of spoken English in our daily lives is something that students are very interested in, especially if they are about to go abroad or are working with foreign clients. In terms of interacting with native English speakers, listening comprehension can be very difficult if not somewhat of a mystery to most. Understanding connected speech is one of the keys to picking up the pace and speaking English quickly.

As you go through class, drop a few examples in when an opportunity arises, adding an extra dimension to things. A list of basic forms of connected speech can be found in the teacher's notes of the topic 'Languages' in Part 2 and the 'complete' version.

Games

If you are interested in adding a few games then find them in Part 2 or the 'complete' version. Make sure that they are relevant to the topic. If you incorporate a game then make sure it's a one off change, especially if you have professionals in your class. Be careful of adding too many games into your lessons. Students will become accustomed to it and expect you to add games every lesson. Continually looking for new games is quite time and energy consuming. The other activities in these lesson plans such as the Power Activities are meant to be equally as fun and energetic, while still centered on the topic and practicing spoken English.

Vivid Description

If you have a 'think of and describe' session then there are a number of ways you can go about this other than just the normal pair work. These will also encourage the learner to be far more focused on their description than usual.

The key to this working well, is to make sure everyone in class changes partners in the same way. Be mindful of this and think about how it is going to run in advance.

Part A: Students to think of one type of (something), for example, one type of sea creature. Its more interesting if you can use the word 'unusual' to make things a bit more difficult, for example, 'Think of an unusual sea creature' or 'Think of an unusual mode of transport'. They should write it down on a piece of paper, for example, 'crab' or 'helicopter'. They should keep it covered so no one else can see it.

Part B: Put your students into pairs. They should then swap their paper with their class mate. They should still keep it covered so no one else can see it. They should then write down six key words to help describe what is on their classmate's piece of paper. Give them two minutes to write down their key words.

Part C: Once they have done this, break up the partnerships; your students should turn to face their neighbour and describe the subject on the paper, for example, 'It lives underwater and has a shell'. Their classmate should guess what it is. This means that you will have to move one student to form a new pairing.

To make it slightly harder, alternatively their classmate could <u>ask yes or no questions</u> until they guess correctly.

Listening and Memory Tester

This is a good way of taking some of the more pedestrian conversations and making them more interesting, for example, 'Talk about your daily schedule'.
It could also be anything from favourite sport, film, music or their opinion on something. Write the question on the whiteboard. You can add simple prompts so that they don't finish too early turning it into a BTQ, for example

'Talk about your daily schedule:
'Get up (When do you get up)? Breakfast (What do you normally have for breakfast)? Go out (When do you go out)? Transport (How do you get to work or college)? Arrive (What time do you arrive)?' and so on.

In pairs each student must answer the question. Its fun if you don't tell them it's a memory game and surprise them later.
Give each student at least two minutes to answer and try and get everyone to finish at the same time.

Once they have done this, get everyone to change partners. Do this by splitting each pair up in opposite directions so each student turns and faces their neighbour. You may need to get one student to stand up and move across the classroom to form their new partnership in order to do this.

Now tell them that this was really a listening exercise and you hope they can remember what was just said. They must then take it in turns going over what their previous partner just told them. Their new partner should listen and ask questions. Both people should have a turn at doing this.

Make a Perfect Sentence
This is an excellent form of clarifying the target language that you will be using for the next discussion. Most students will tell you they know what something means and then ask their classmate as soon as you start the activity. This removes this element.

Pick target language from your list on the whiteboard and ask one student to form a 'perfect' sentence with it. If they make an error then ask the class to briefly correct it. Don't dwell on it for too long as not to embarrass whoever made the mistake.
You can also do this at key times such as before break or the end of class.

Future and Past Tense Reminders
All of your students will be able to speak in the present tense. However, you really need to focus their attention on using the future and past otherwise they will almost immediately forget the aim when they start talking. Reminders are added in brackets in each lesson plan. These are meant to underline the importance of really focusing your students at the task at hand. Here are a few ways you can do this.

1: Before starting, tell an anecdote of something you did in the past only do it in the present tense. "Last year I go to Xiamen on holiday. It is a really great time, though is too hot. There are so many people on the beach I have to go somewhere else". Alternately talk about something you will be doing in the future. Students should correct you while you speak.

2: Before starting, ask one student (A) to think of a verb in its base form. The next student (B) must put it into the past tense. They should now think of another verb (base form). The next student along (C) should put it into the past and so on. If you have ten students or less, you may have time to go round the class twice. The second time around will go really smoothly with no prompting from the teacher.

3: Before starting, tell the class that you will be switching tenses while they are talking. Inform them exactly what you will be doing and what they should do. Do an ICQ as some students may think they have to switch partner aswell as switching tenses. Some may stop speaking altogether when you say 'switch' thinking their partner should be doing the work instead. A minute or so into the activity, shout "CHANGE: PRESENT TENSE!" and they must speak in the present. A minute or so later, shout "NOW CHANGE: PAST TENSE!" and so on.

4: Put people into groups of three. If you can't put everyone into threes then also add one pair. One student must answer the question in whatever tense while their classmates listen. If they make an error with their tenses their classmates should hit the table. The person doing the talking must correct themselves or if they can't, then their partners can make a suggestion. You can do this form of correction with anything.

Can't Say 'Yes' or 'No'
A nice activity you can inject into any discussion that involves asking questions.
In pairs, the person answering must not reply using 'yes' of 'no'.

You can set up an activity especially for this towards the end of class if you need to inject some life back into the proceedings. If you do this as a separate activity, as soon as someone uses 'yes' or 'no' then they must switch partners so the person asking the questions is now answering and so on. Yes or no answers questions begin with:

Is it/she/he/that/this, Am I, Are you/they/these/we, Can you/they/it/she/he,
Was it/his/her(s)/she/he/I, Were they/the/you, Have you/they/the, Has your/she/he
Do you/they, Does she/he, Did I/it/she/he/you/they/these,
Can I/we/she/he/it/you/they/these, Could I/we/she/he/it/you/they/these, May I
Will I/we/she/he/it/you/they/these, Would I/we/she/he/it/you/they/these

If you want to give your class a hand, then write these prompts on the white board:
'Is, are, can, was, were, have, has, do, does, did, can, could, may, will, would'.
Quickly run over each word and ask them to make one 'yes' or 'no' question from each.

Ask to Borrow Something
This is a very simple activity I throw in at the end of a lesson if it has been particularly quiet or you have had low ability students who have been struggling. This will bring the class back to life before they go home and give confidence to those who have found things difficult. It is infact a mini roleplay in pairs:

<u>Person A:</u> Ask to borrow something from your friend on the desk (pen, phone, eraser etc). You really need it. Never give up.
<u>Person B:</u> Make excuses not to lend it.

You can easily switch partners and repeat the exercise.

End of Class Boardwork
Decide whether or not you are going to do this before you start your lesson. During class make sure you fill your board with vocabulary. With five minutes remaining get everyone to look at the white board and remember what and where everything is. Time them for one minute. Make them all turn around with their eyes closed. While they aren't looking remove one word. Ask them to open their eyes and face the board. Ask one person to tell you which word is missing and ensure their friends don't help them. Repeat the activity only remove two words and so on.

Smart English

TEFL Discussion Questions & Activities – China

Complete Book of PDF Printables

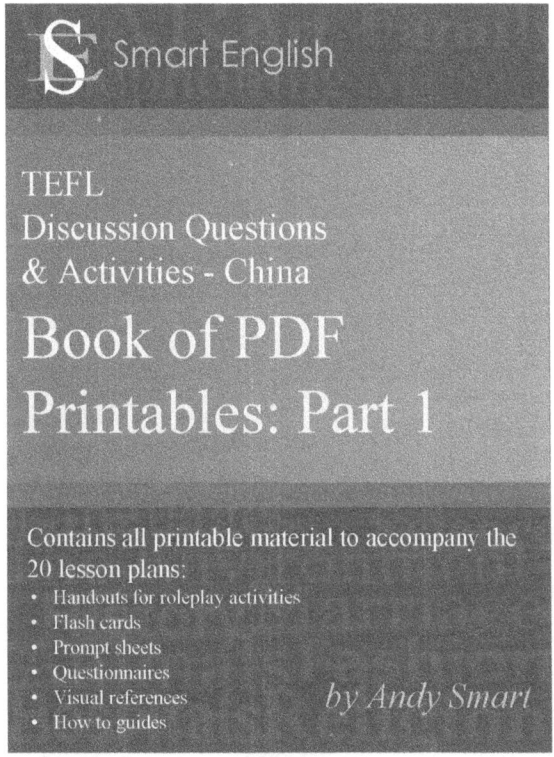

This book is designed to be a helpful time saver for printing off the various worksheets, roleplays, handouts and flashcards. It is a free package designed to make your life easier. All the topics are bookmarked on the left of the screen so they can be accessed quickly. They have the same order and numbering as Kick-Ass Lesson Plans - TEFL Discussion Questions and Activities China Part 1

To receive the book, just send an e-mail to me at smartenglish@hotmail.co.uk anytime. Please copy and paste this PIN to your letter:

SMARTENGLISH: A01 – SJY2568

www.ingramcontent.com/pod-product-compliance
Lightning Source LLC
Chambersburg PA
CBHW081128170426

43197CB00017B/2785